I0828157

Creations:

Looking at Nature and History

Paintings by Frank O'Cain

DEDICATION

To my dear wife, Rebekah, who provides laughter and magic and support for my creative endeavors.

ACKNOWLEDGMENTS

I thank Stephen Durkee for his support, expertise and graphic sensibilities in laying out this catalog. His generosity in time and patience was instrumental in its manifestation.

Softcover ISBN 979-8-9888717-0-5

Epub ISBN 979-8-9888717-1-2

ARTIST STATEMENT

Like Cezanne, Hans Hofmann and others before me, I begin with an inspiration from the world around me. Ideas and inspirations for my works can derive from the radiant light of nature or the rattling bones of history. I abstract from the raven, standing stones in Scotland, ancient structures and legends left by unknown races as well as inspirations from nature that I see during daily life. Once I have firmly embraced an idea, I move it into the two dimensional space of the canvas and begin to craft an image that will pull the viewer into my world for a satisfying and meaningful interaction with the idea and the art.

My painting derives from a constant study and practice of historic and modern techniques, including long-forgotten techniques from the fifteenth-century. This may result in some works having a hundred separate glazes. Based upon my belief that good craftsmanship is the basis of good art, I only use the best materials. The strongest elements in my work are light, color and spatial structure. However, I never approach a work of art by rote or habit. Each painting is approached as a separate act of creation.

In addition to the influences of my many teachers, friends and students, my approach to abstraction builds upon a lineage of artists including Rembrandt, De Kooning, Franz Kline, Motherwell, Hofmann,the Japanese calligraphists and Zen painters and, especially, Cezanne.

https://frank-ocain-yxxj.squarespace.com

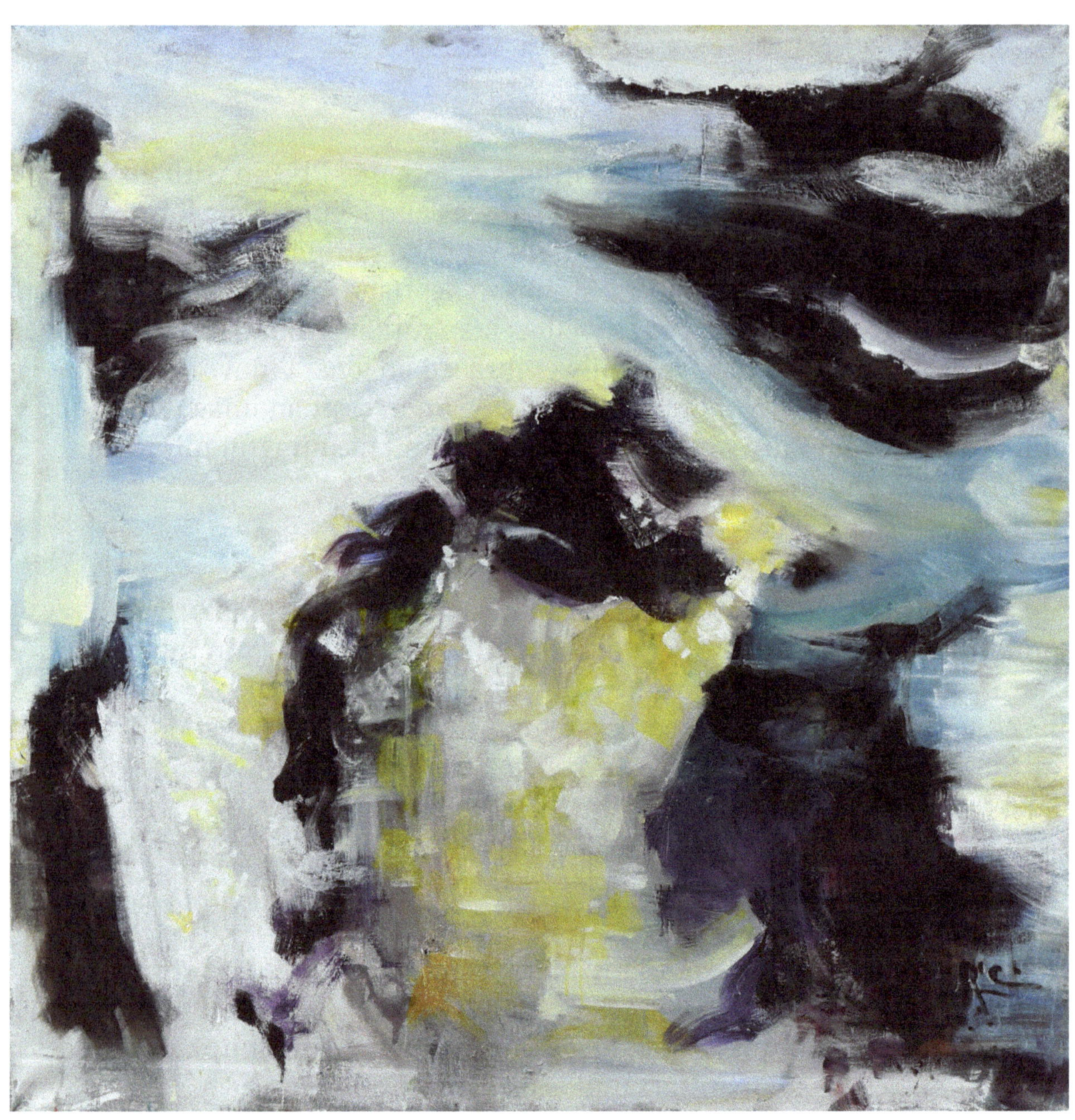

^Songs My Ancestors Sang		
Waiting III	2018	60" x 60½"
> France Remembered		
Sensations of France - Night Flight	1999	59 ½" x 72

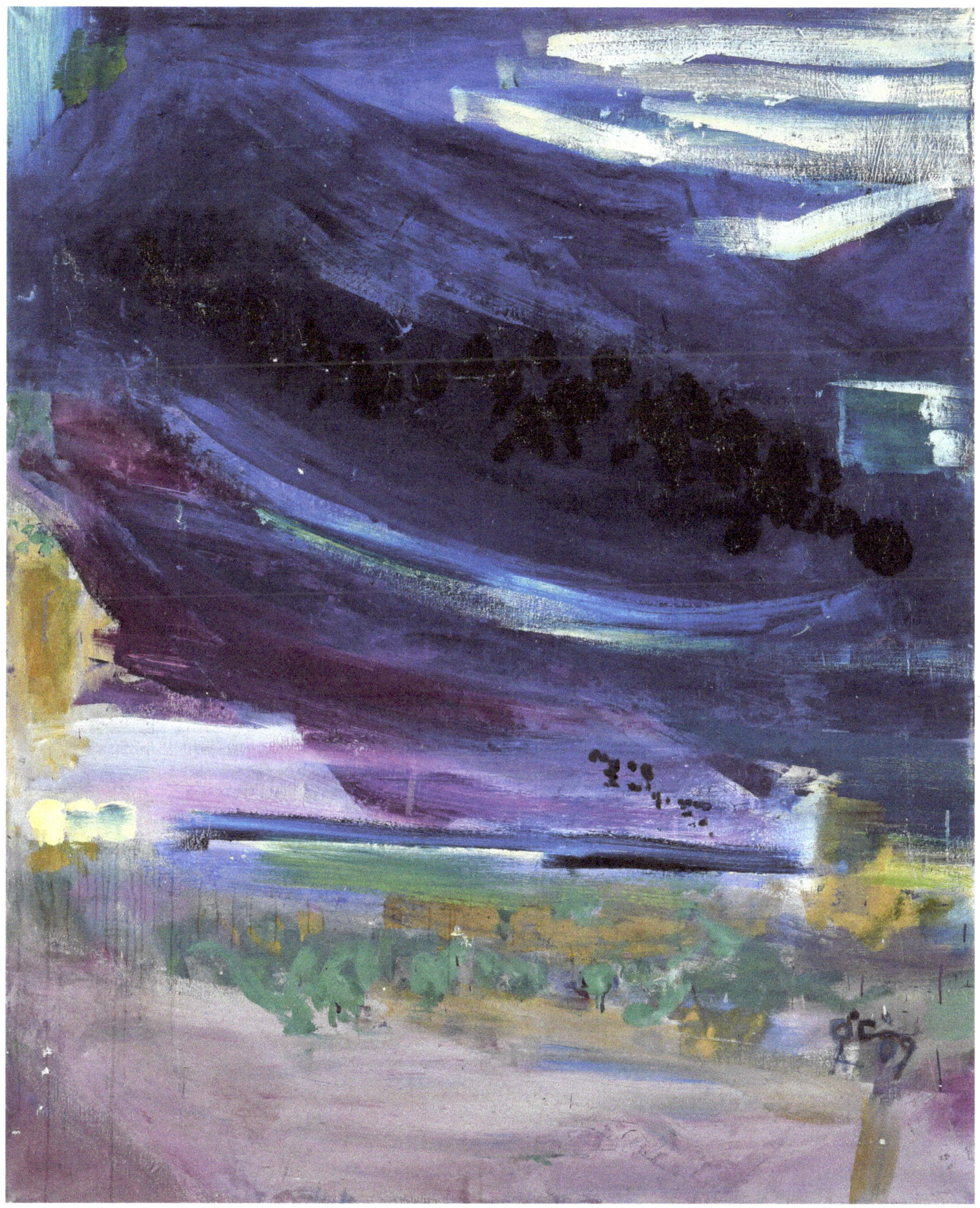

Action of one's experience
becomes the new reality

Each painting has tension on the surface
Energy being pulled into us
The crow as competitor
We watch We see We are amazed

Heildegard Dancing with Bach 2013 48" x 60"

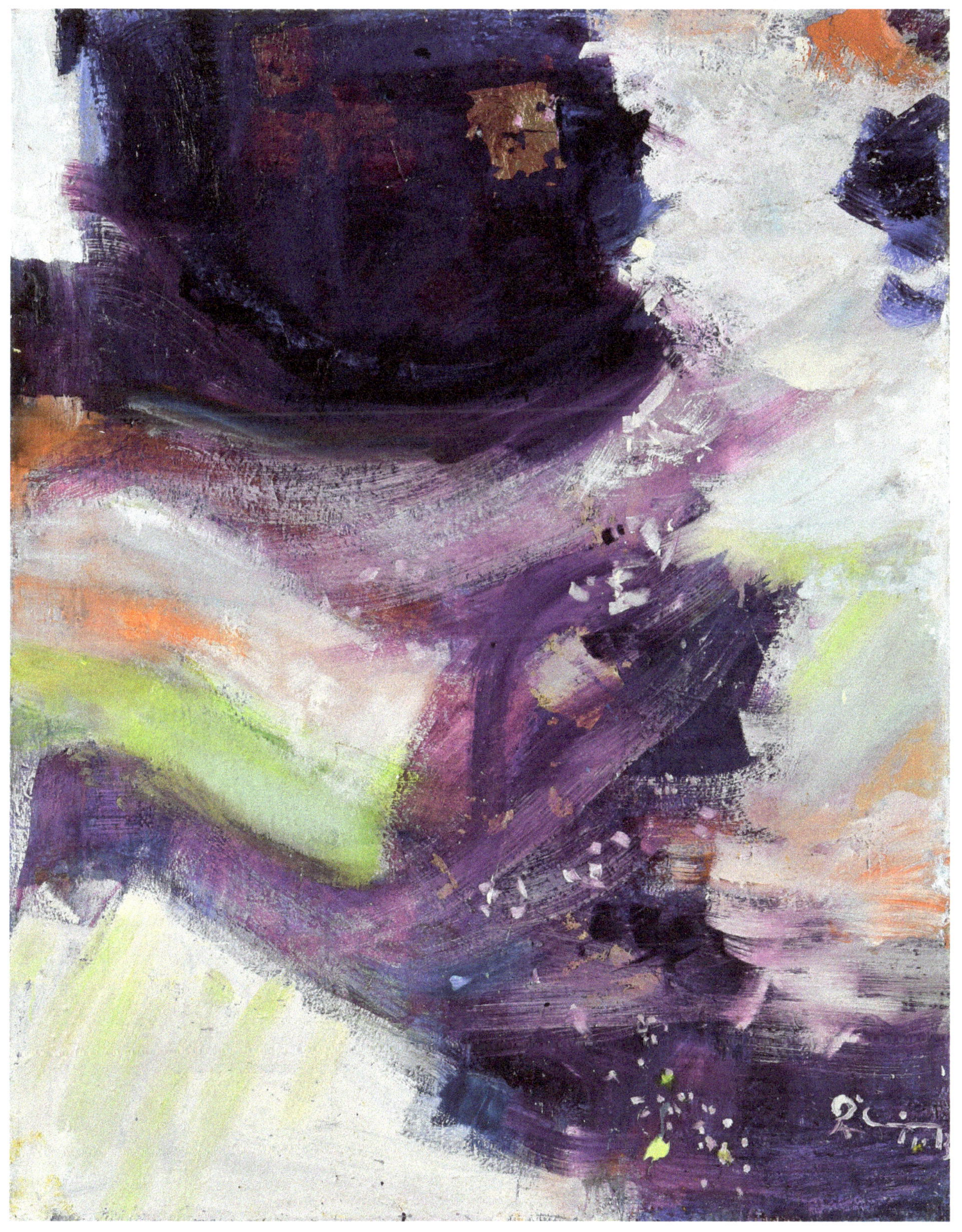

STONES

There upon dark places forms reach out
to
minds playing like some all knowing magic moment
where so many have ask
where do these pieces of our
past come from

How often we have been where these images of our
secret needs have gone and brought to each time
a question
where are we where are we
silent
standing in the path of winds and rain
torrents of feeling
as
those times a sudden
our flesh press
the soil mingling with the sky
these stones begin to dance before us
connecting the time we know with the time we
have forgotten

Till small glimpses
swell and give to us a
cold chill
a sudden knowing
we are
we have
we must continue this voyage from star to earth
or we are the pole of times creation
and
here the forms still stand and give us
a direction
a place to ask
question
and feel

Will
a small part remember the how
and will the understanding
give us our voyage back.

Frank O'Cain

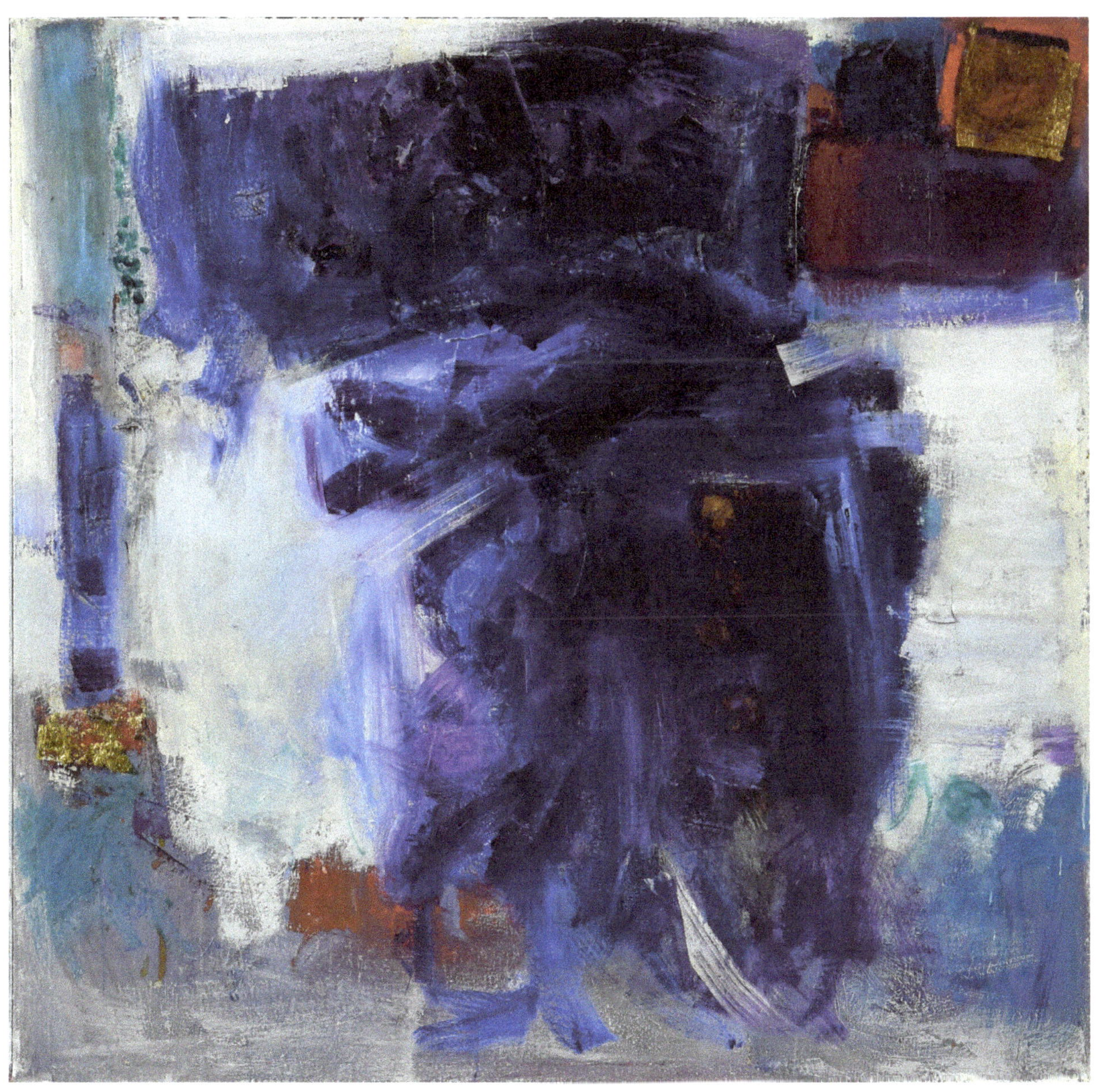

Power of Stone I 1995 48” x 50”

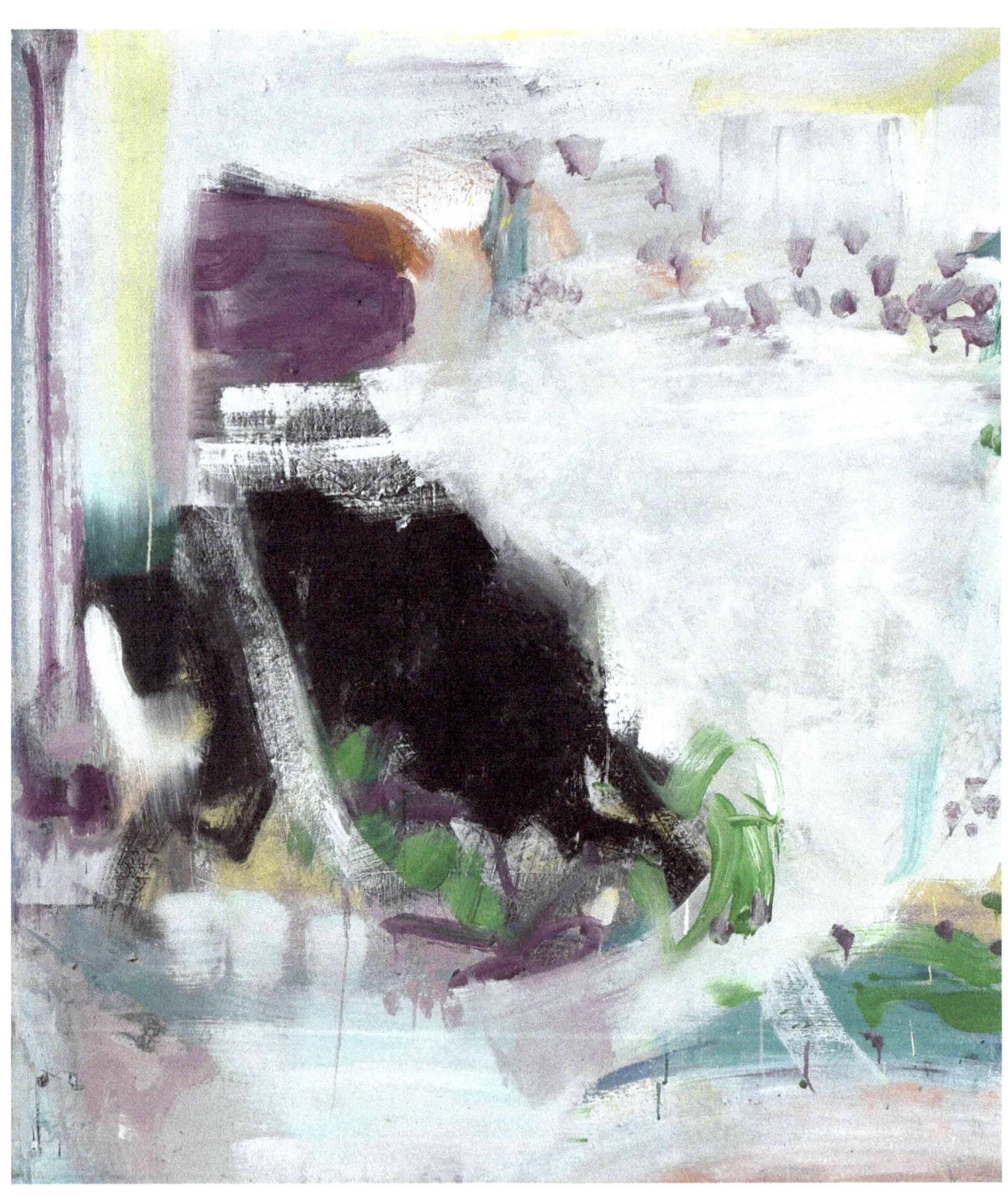

Songs My Ancestors Sang
Shapes in Passing 2002 91 ½" x 51"

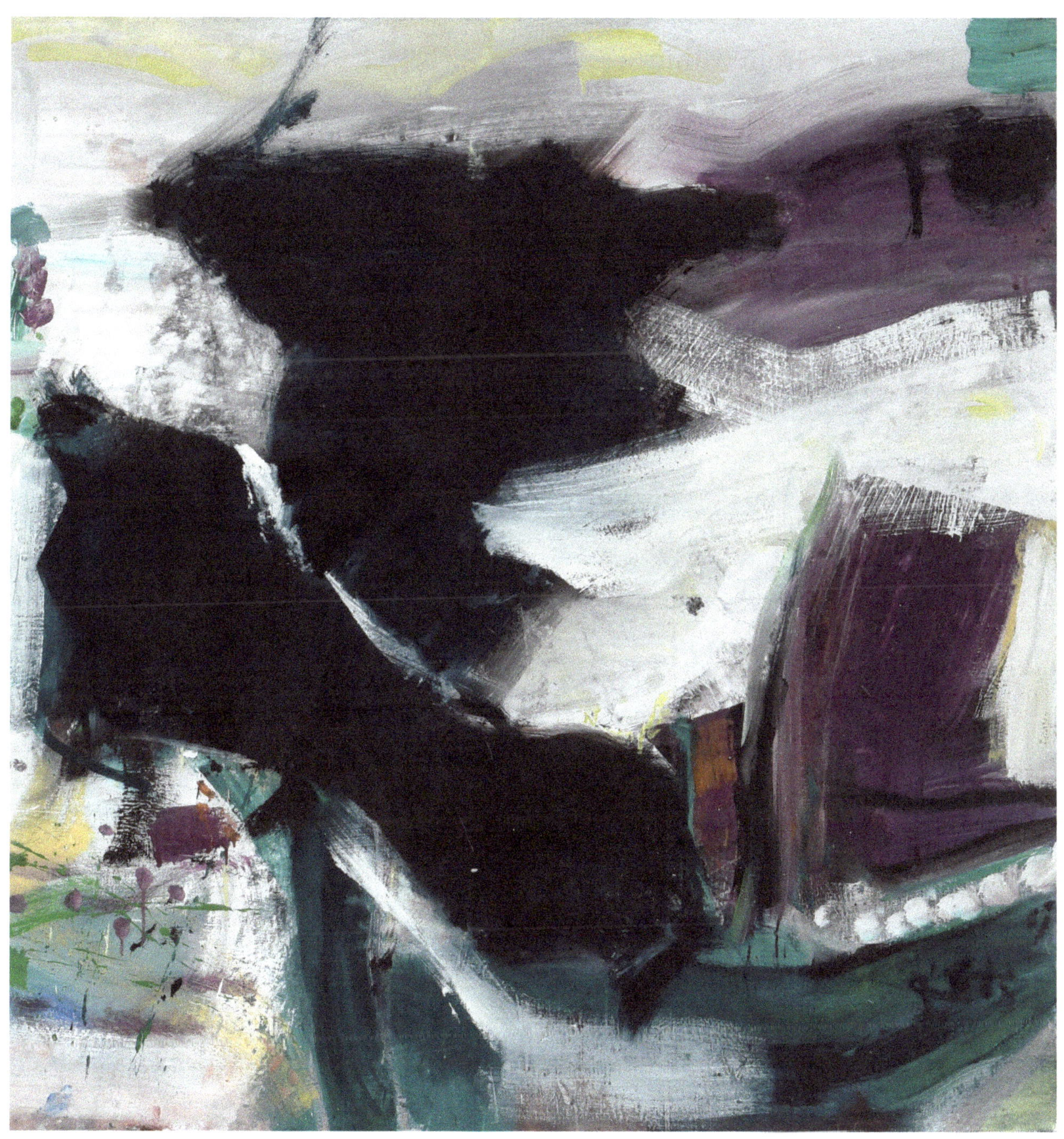

From who we are in memory

Flow from land to sea

Light comes from within

Moments of thought while looking at the past

Changing light

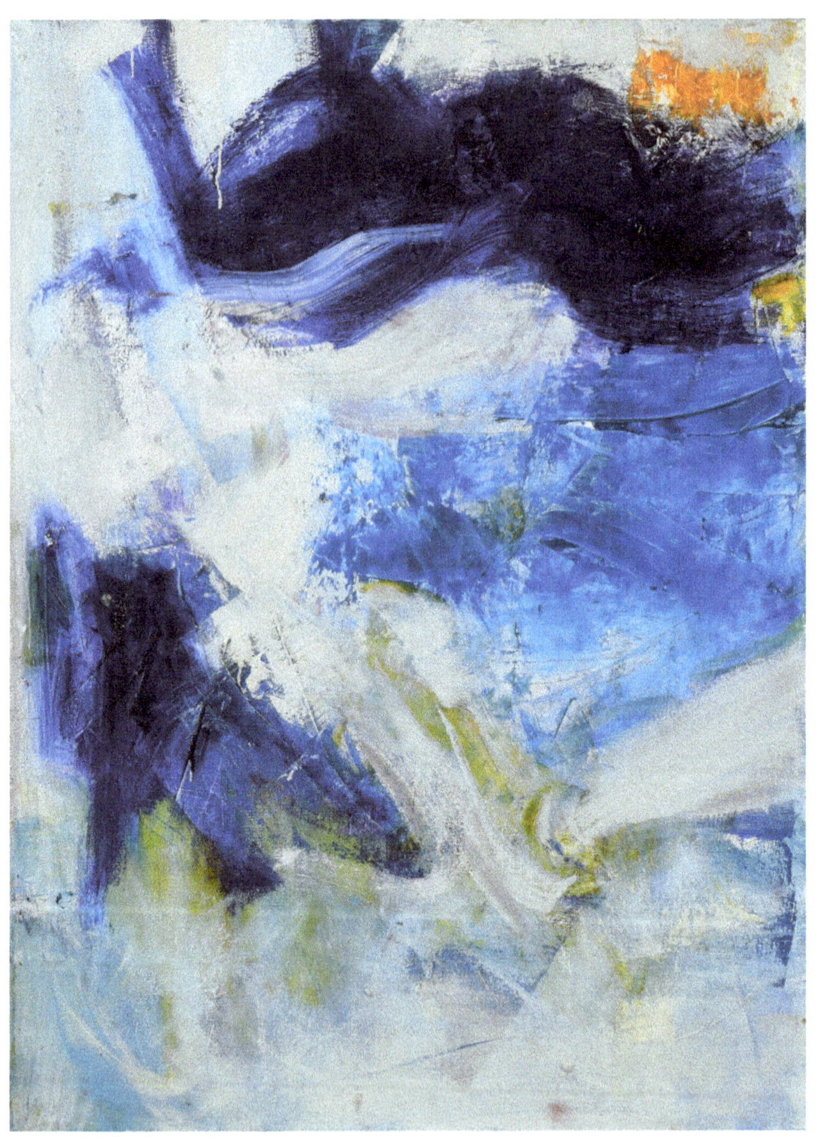

Songs My Ancestors Sang
Song of Sea and Sky 2012 36" x 36"

>Songs My Ancestors Sang
Power of Stone II 2009 48" x 60"

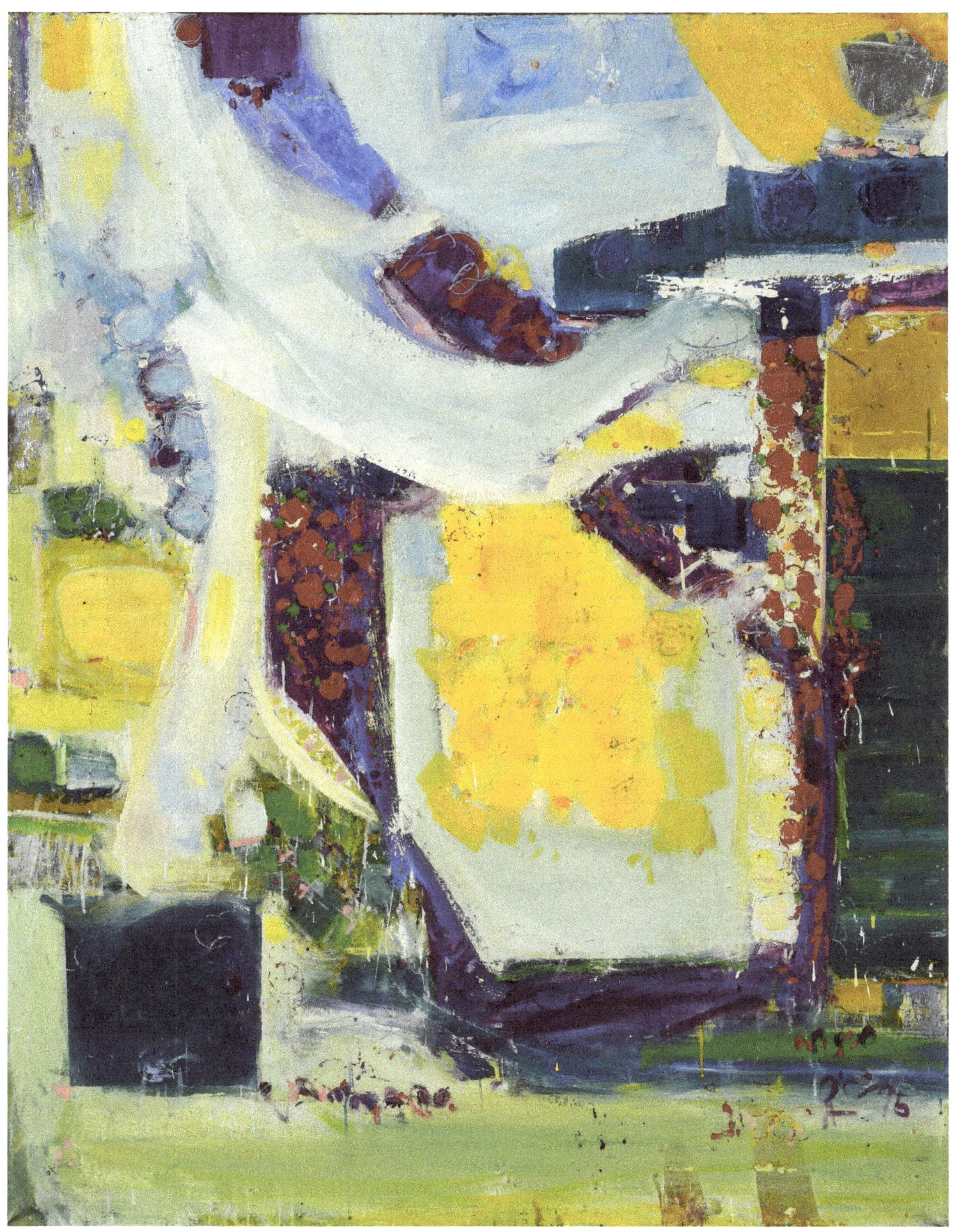

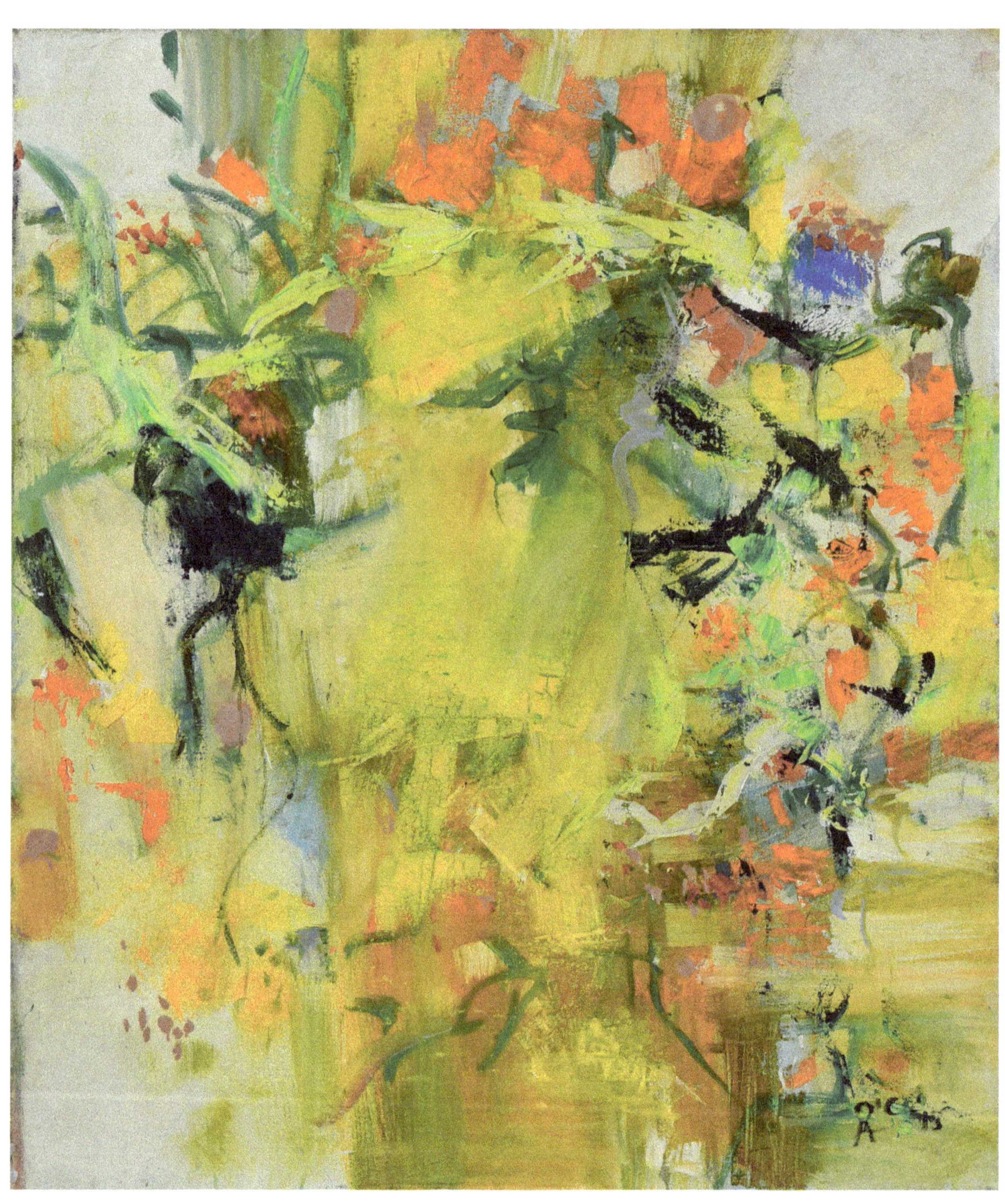

^Spring's Winter Study of Light	2018	40" x 50
>Songs My Ancestors Sang Rejected	2013	40" x 56"^

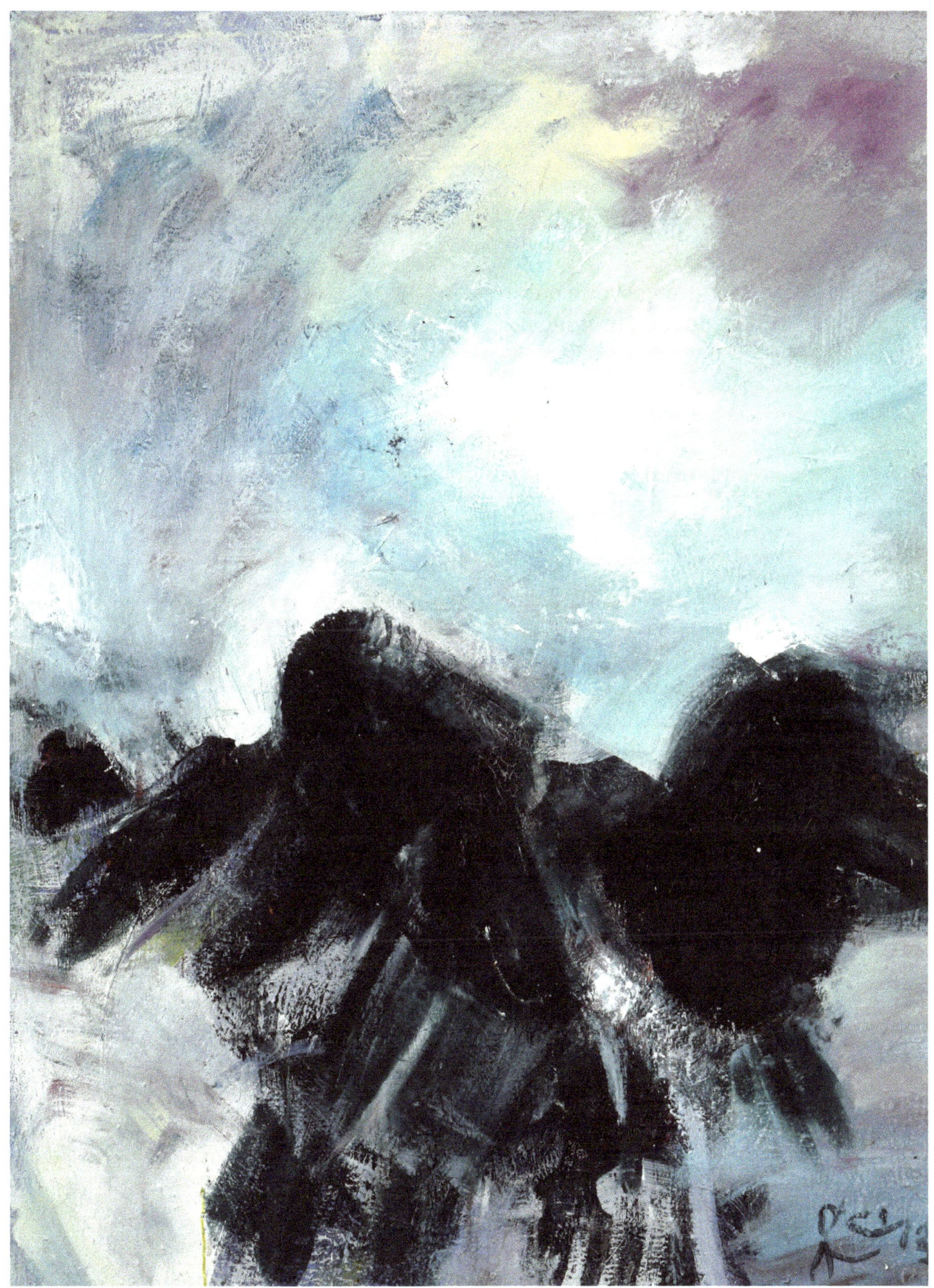

LAND RHYMES

Light clinging
to
blue, pink, violet
tones
vibrating beyond our eyes
singing to our minds.

Kiss, listen and laugh
as we should
one with the dance nature provides
and recall
when the music stops.

So allow the Soul to bring about
its needs
and dance while we may
and
struggle to give it a fresh tomorrow.

Frank O'Cain

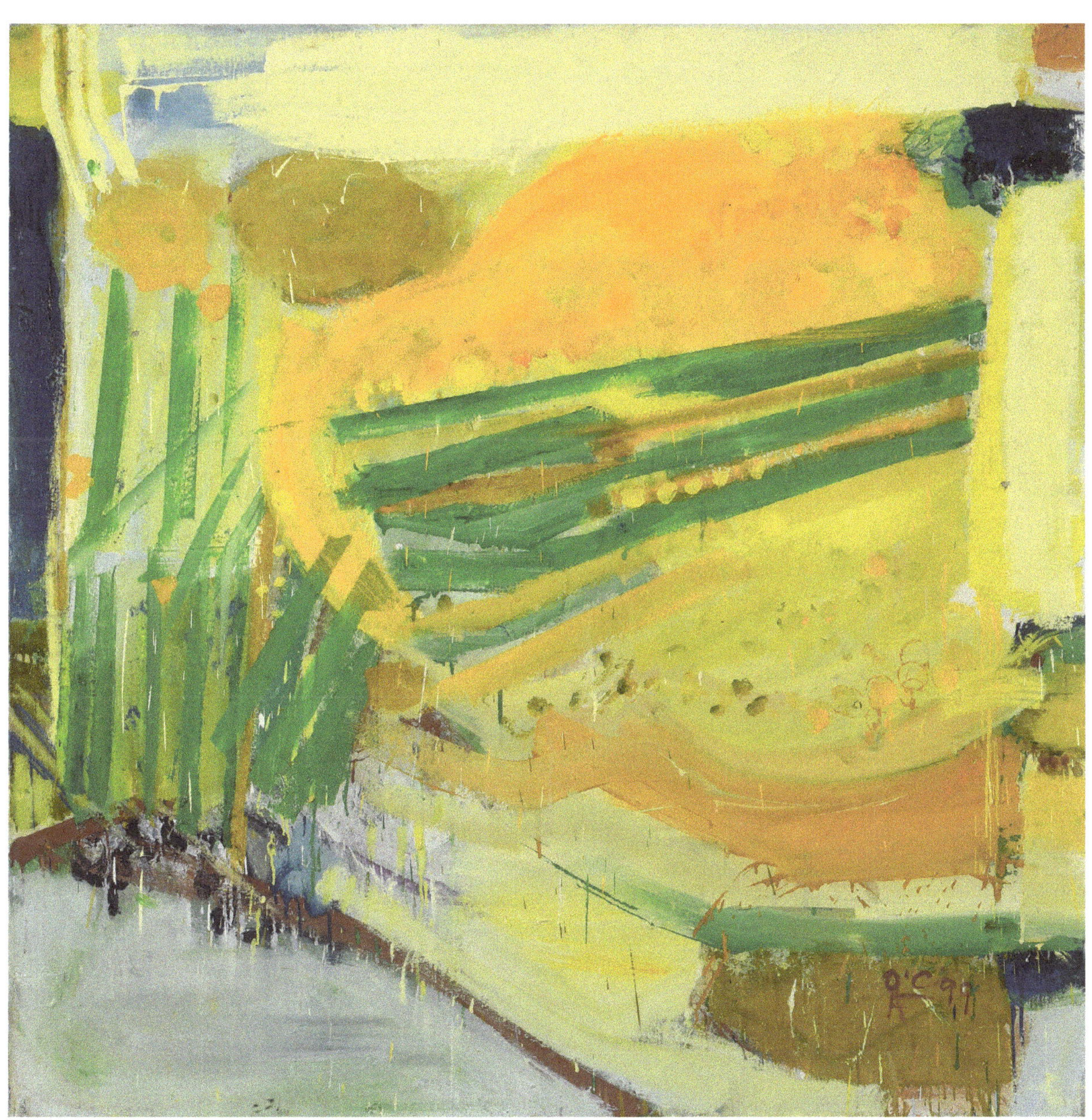

France Remembered
Sensations III 1999 65" x 64"

We come from water and some of us return

Seasons

Explosion of volcano – Staffa

Sound and energy of Spain

Early explorations of sensation

Songs My Ancestors Sang
Voices from Beneath 2002 60" x 72" two panels

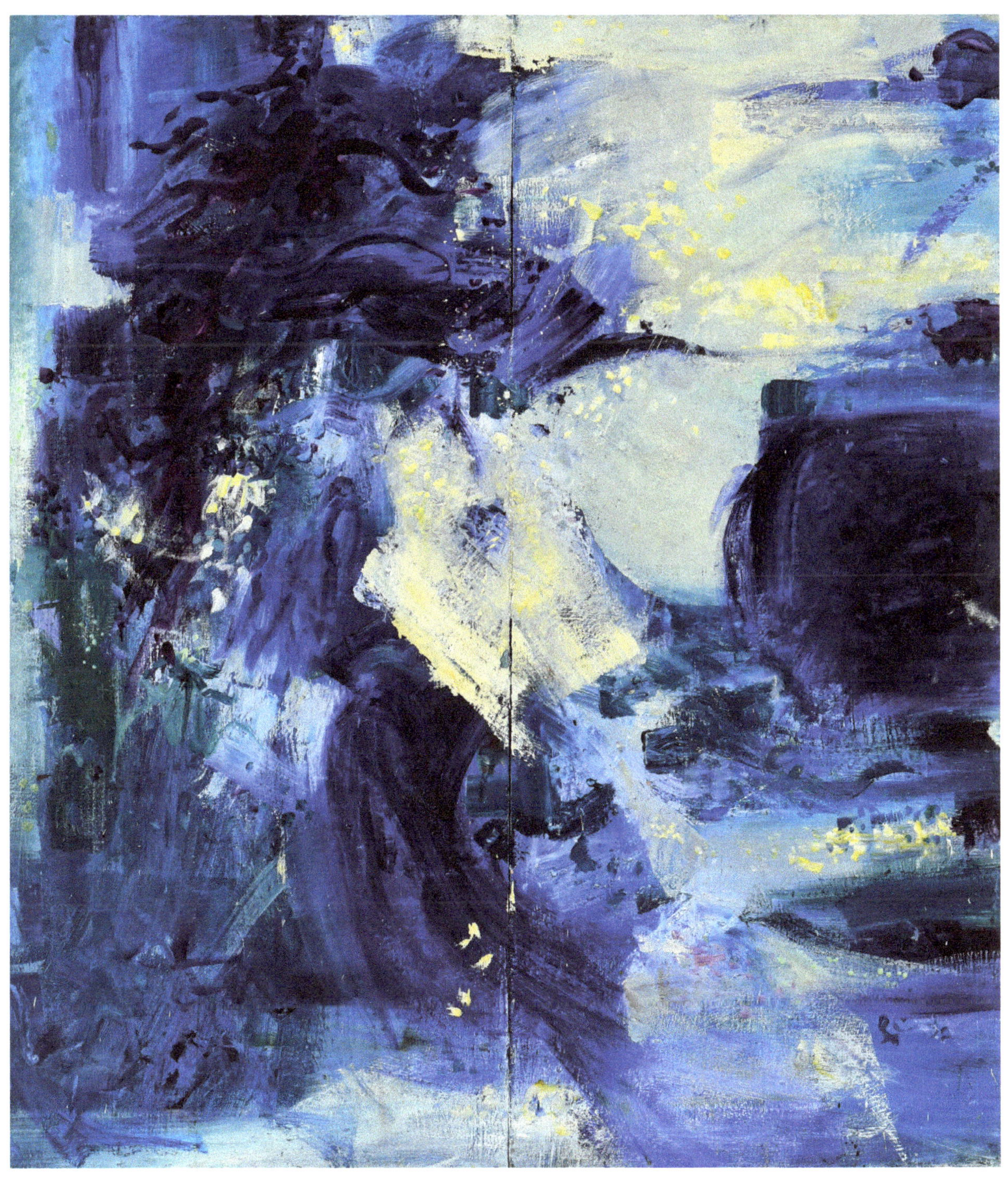

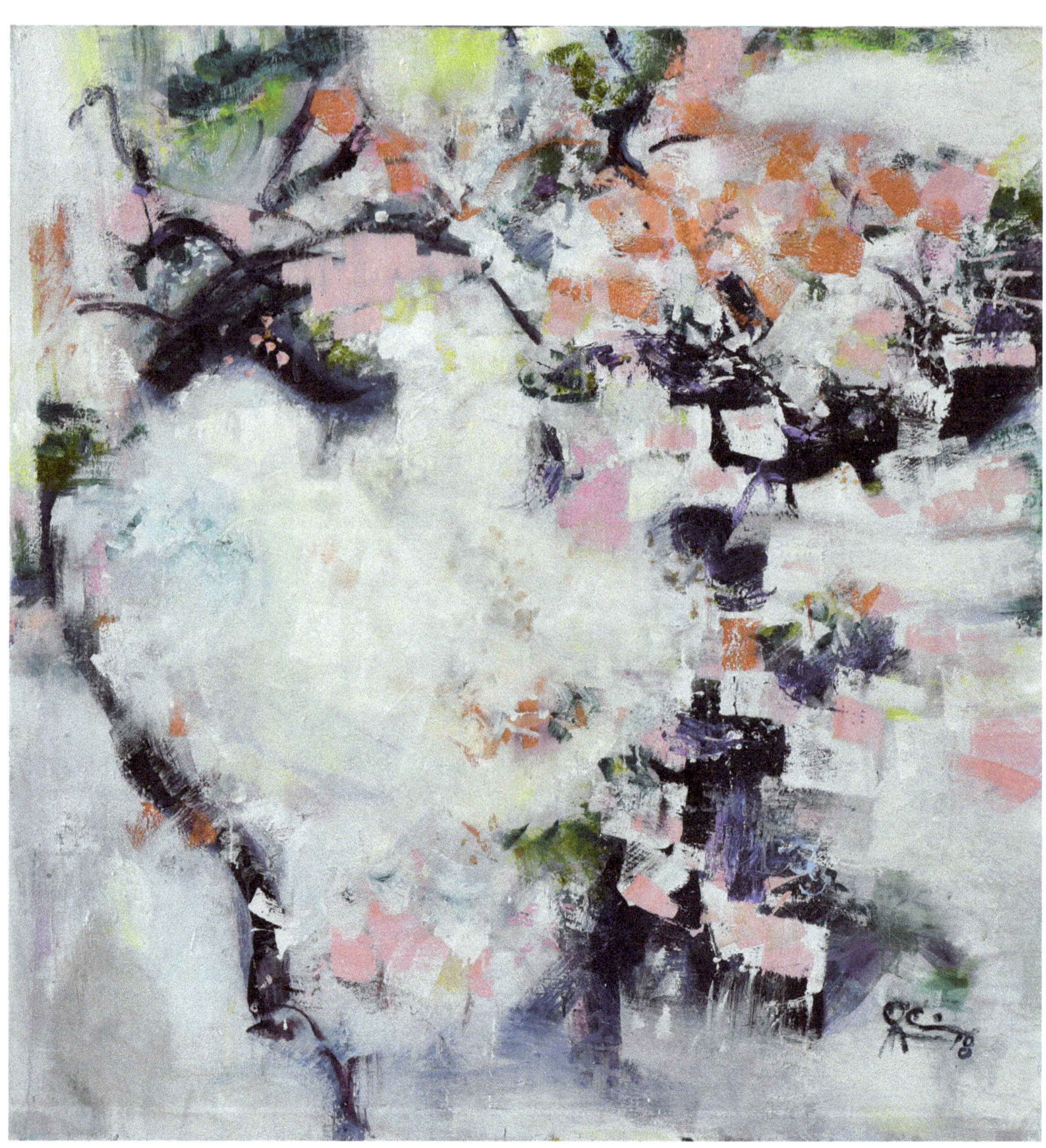

Spring's Winter Opus I	2018	44" x 50"
>Songs My Ancestors Sang Staffa I	2002	50" x 72"

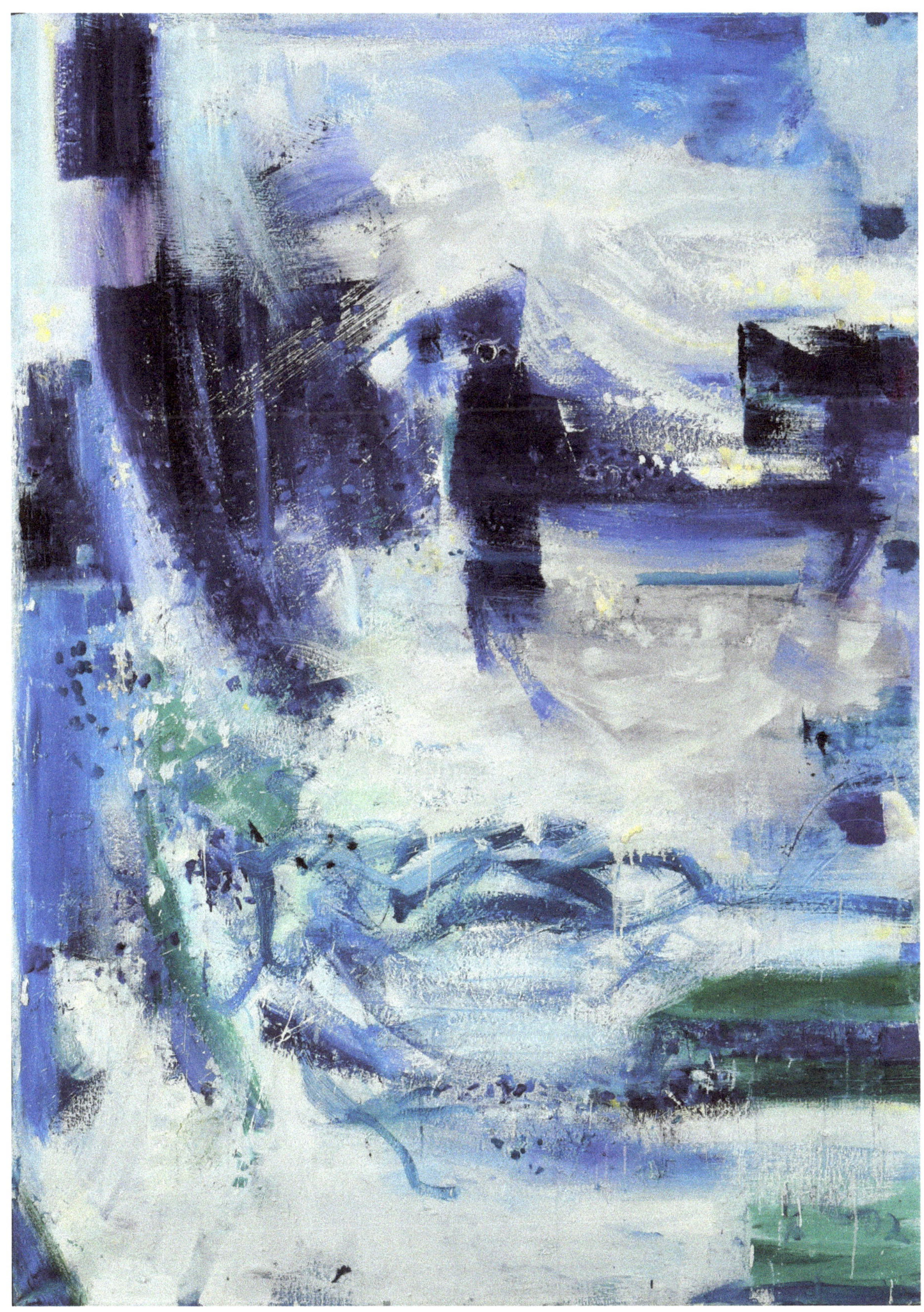

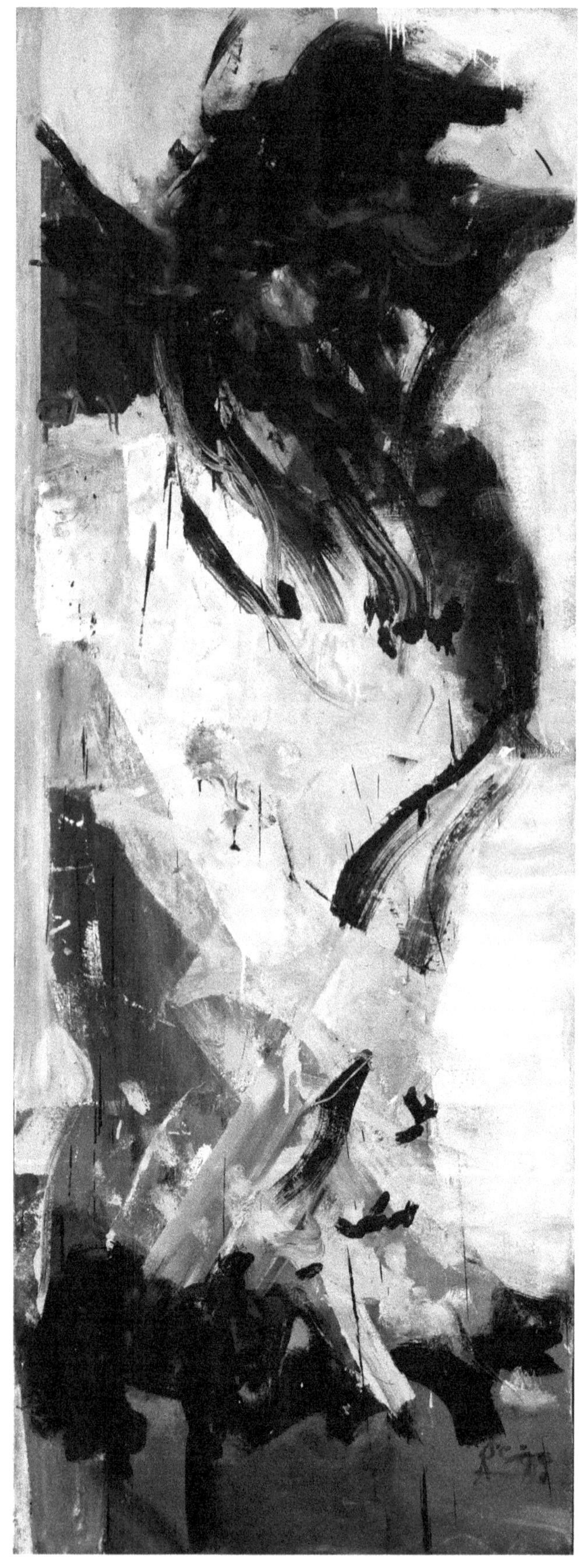

SOUL CATCHER

Being
 In present
 Seeing.
Shapes entangled
 Black swerving.
Until two
 Become one.
This moment
 Brought the
 Continuum
 of
 Need to fulfill.
As the action
 Spent out into
 My mind
 Ancient
 Cries
 Began.
The hordes in
 Aftermath
 of Battle.
Deep in the
 Blood that
 Flows.
Rushing into the Crows
 Own feeding
 Upon the field of
 Fallen warriors.
Stealing from
 The now
 The Soul
 They so much Craved.

Frank O'Cain

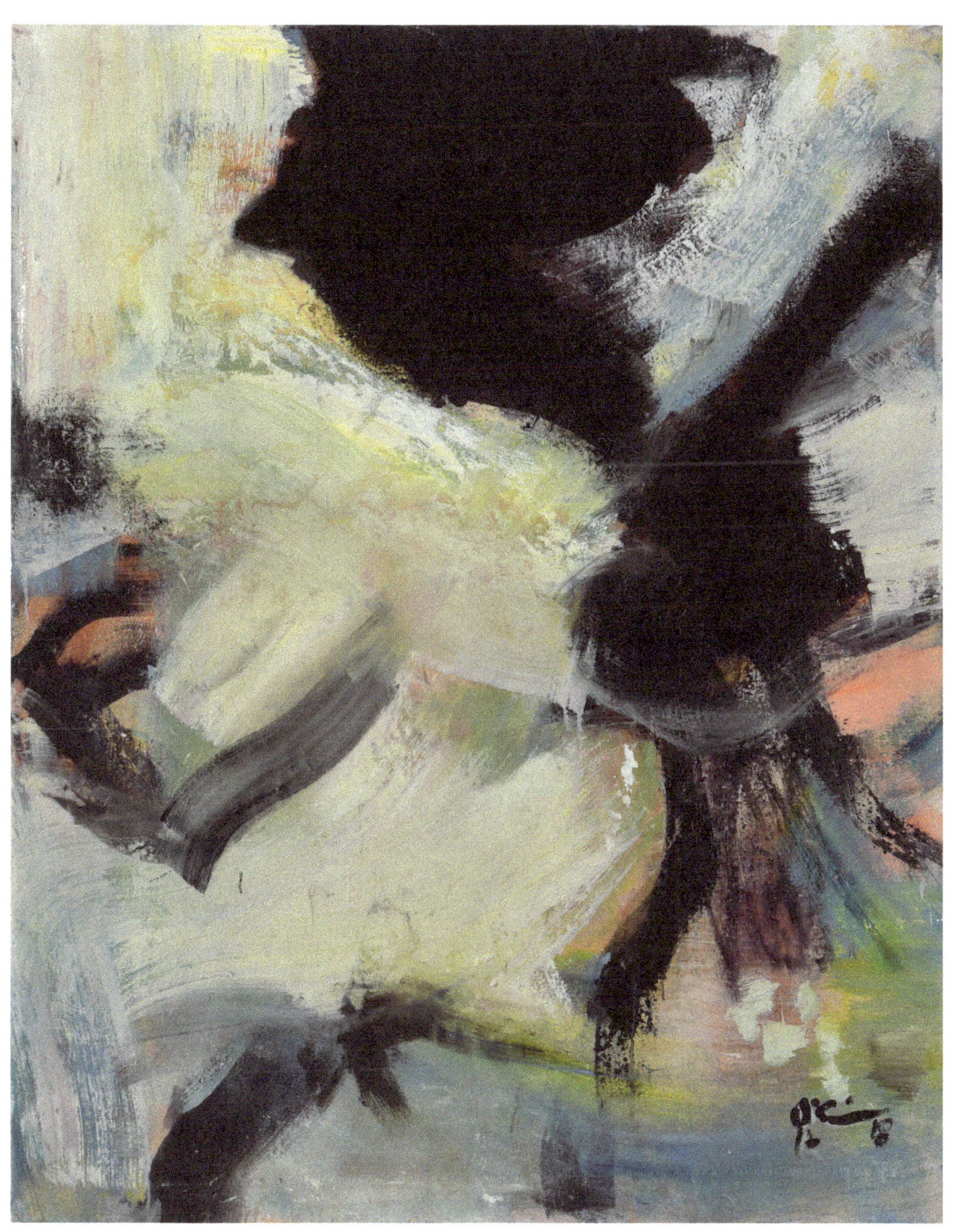

<Songs My Ancestors Sang
Soul Catcher 1994 30" x 79"

^Songs My Ancestors Sang
The Waiting Field 2018 40" x 50"

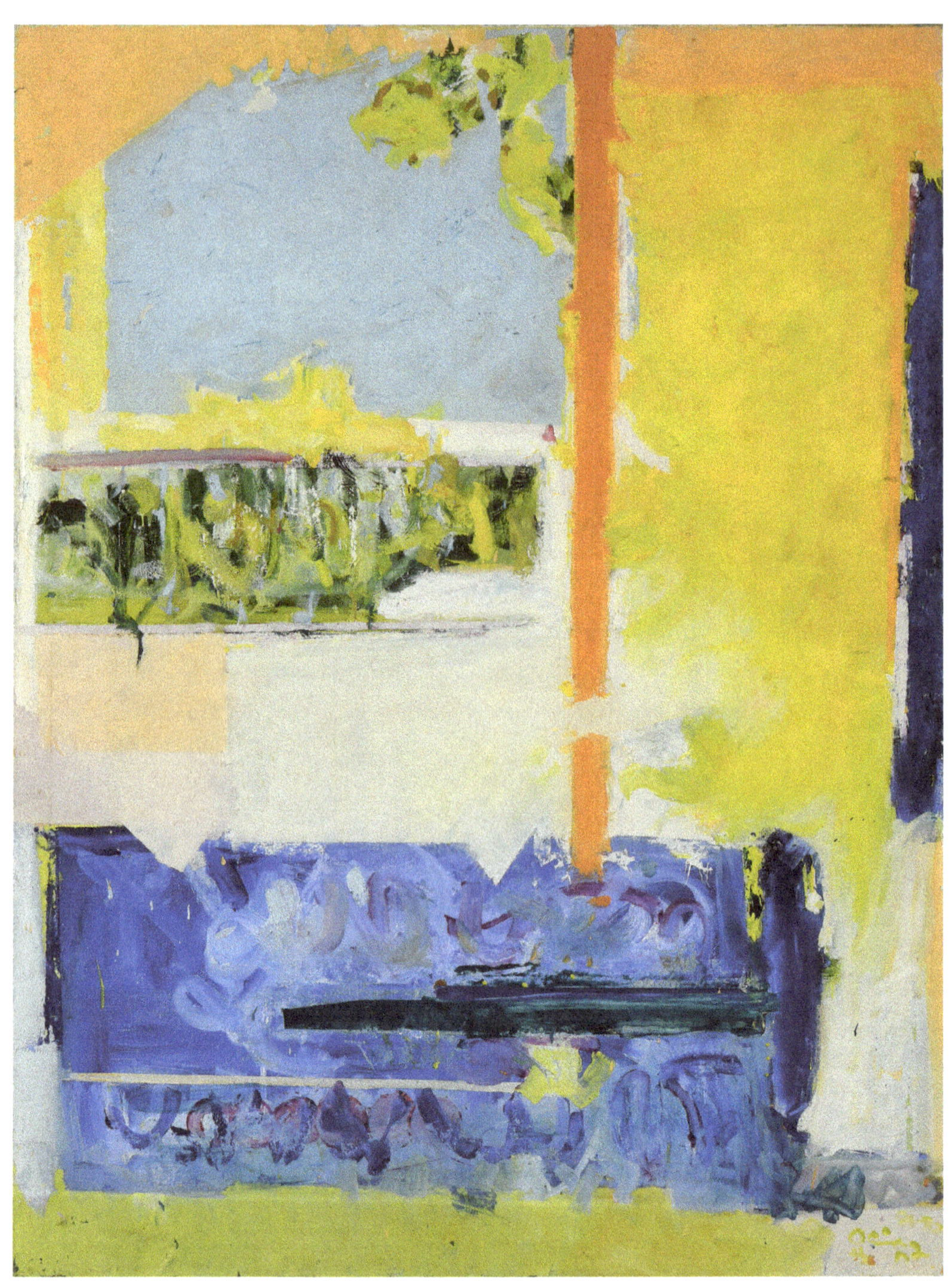

^Changes I	1979	50" x 72"
>Spanish Rhythm	1995	48" x 56"

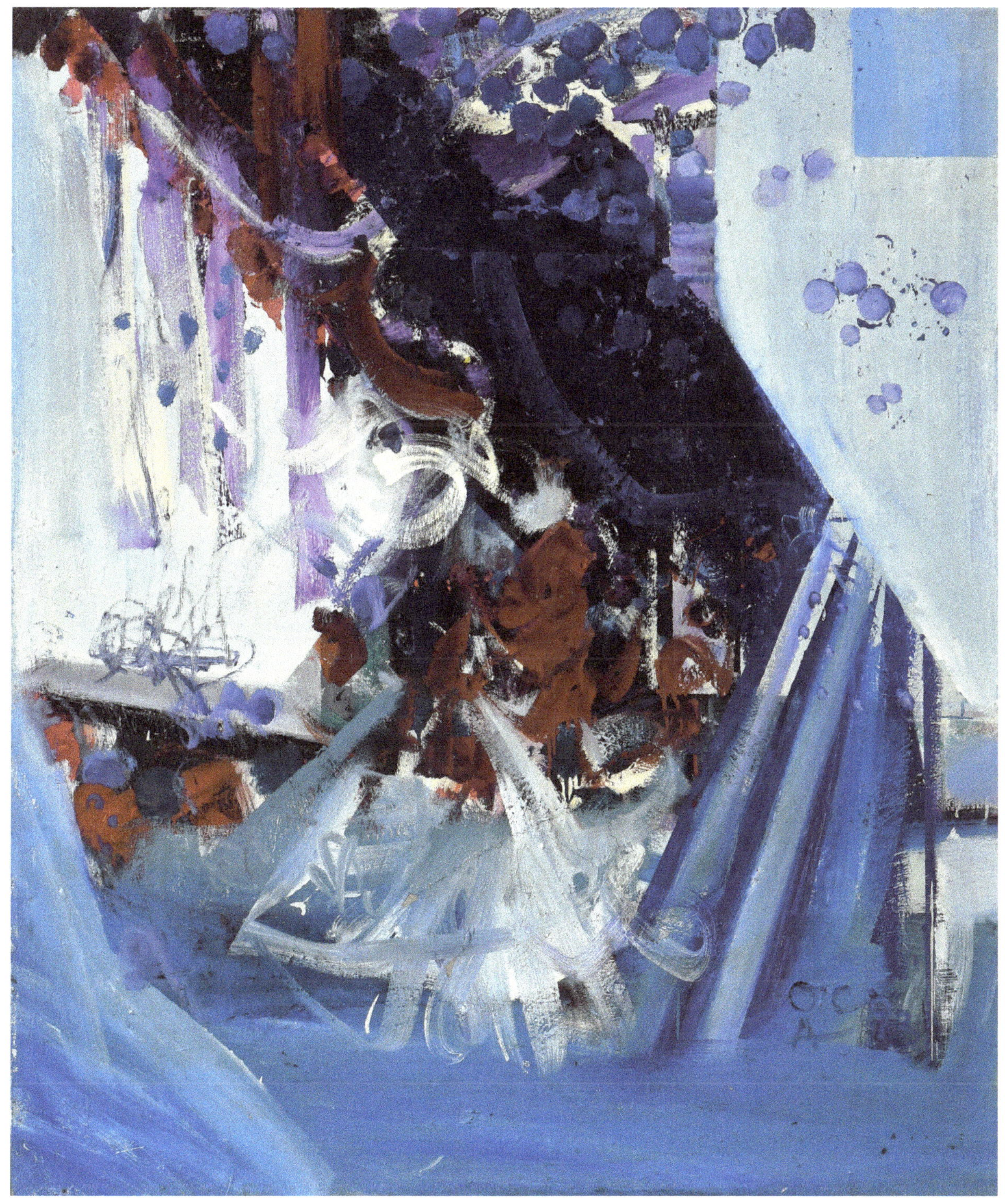

Sensual France

The land needs to feed the eye to enhance the soul

To find moments transfixed and in need of rest

Sitting in nature

France Remembered
Rememberiing Opus I 1999 65" x 64"

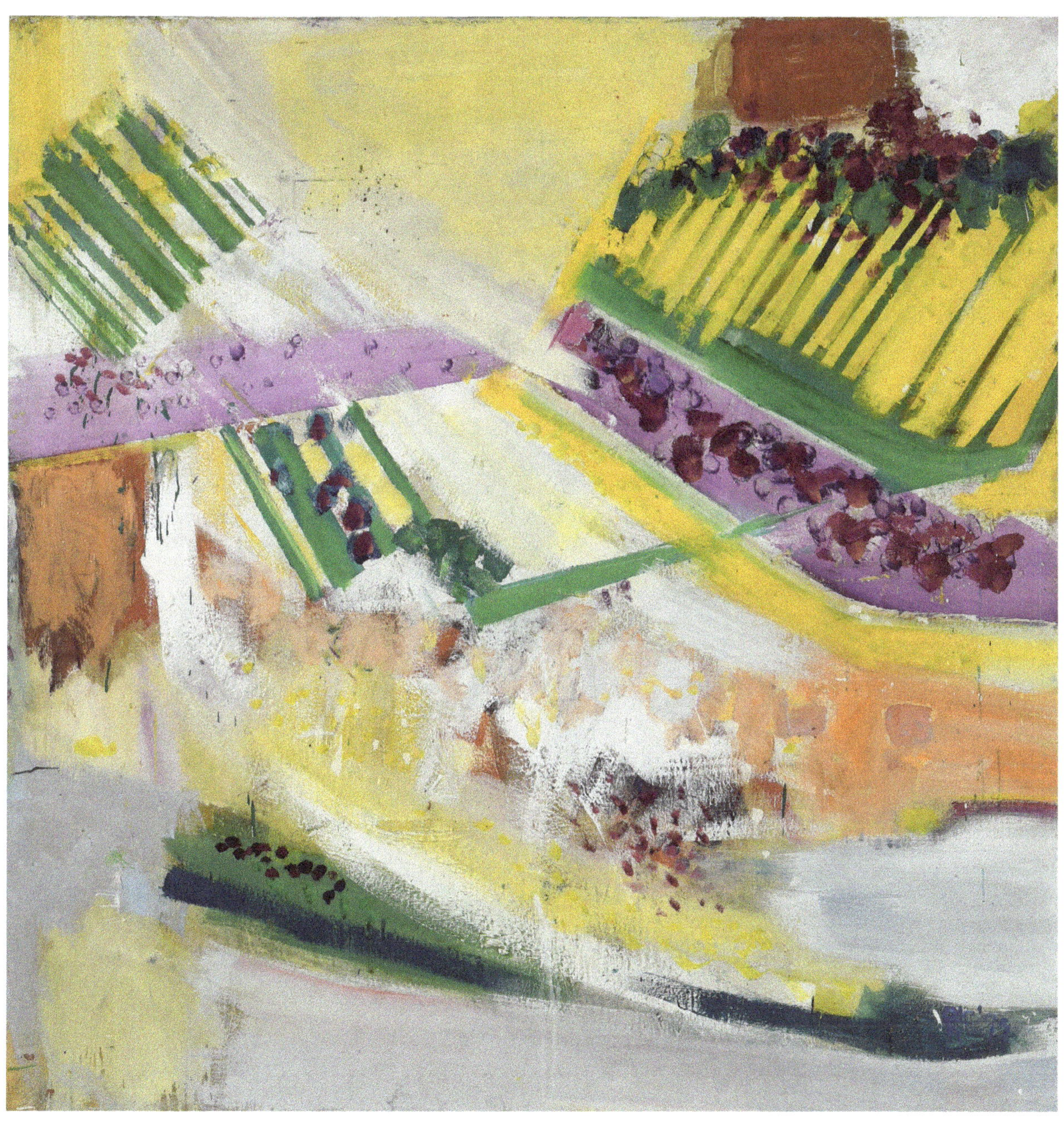

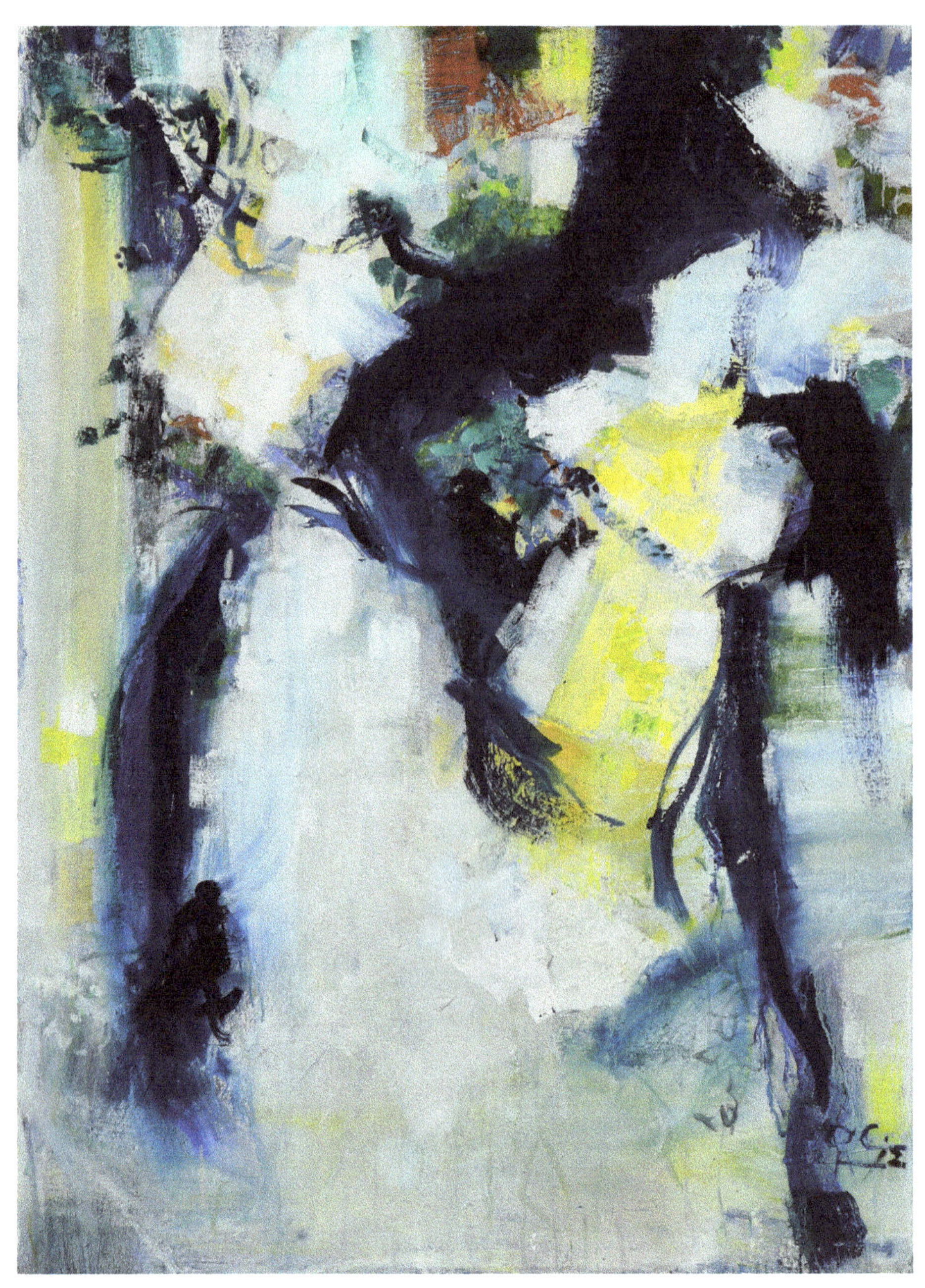

Esoteric Motions	1993	48" x 56"
Songs My Ancestors Sang Dance in May	2003	65" x 72"

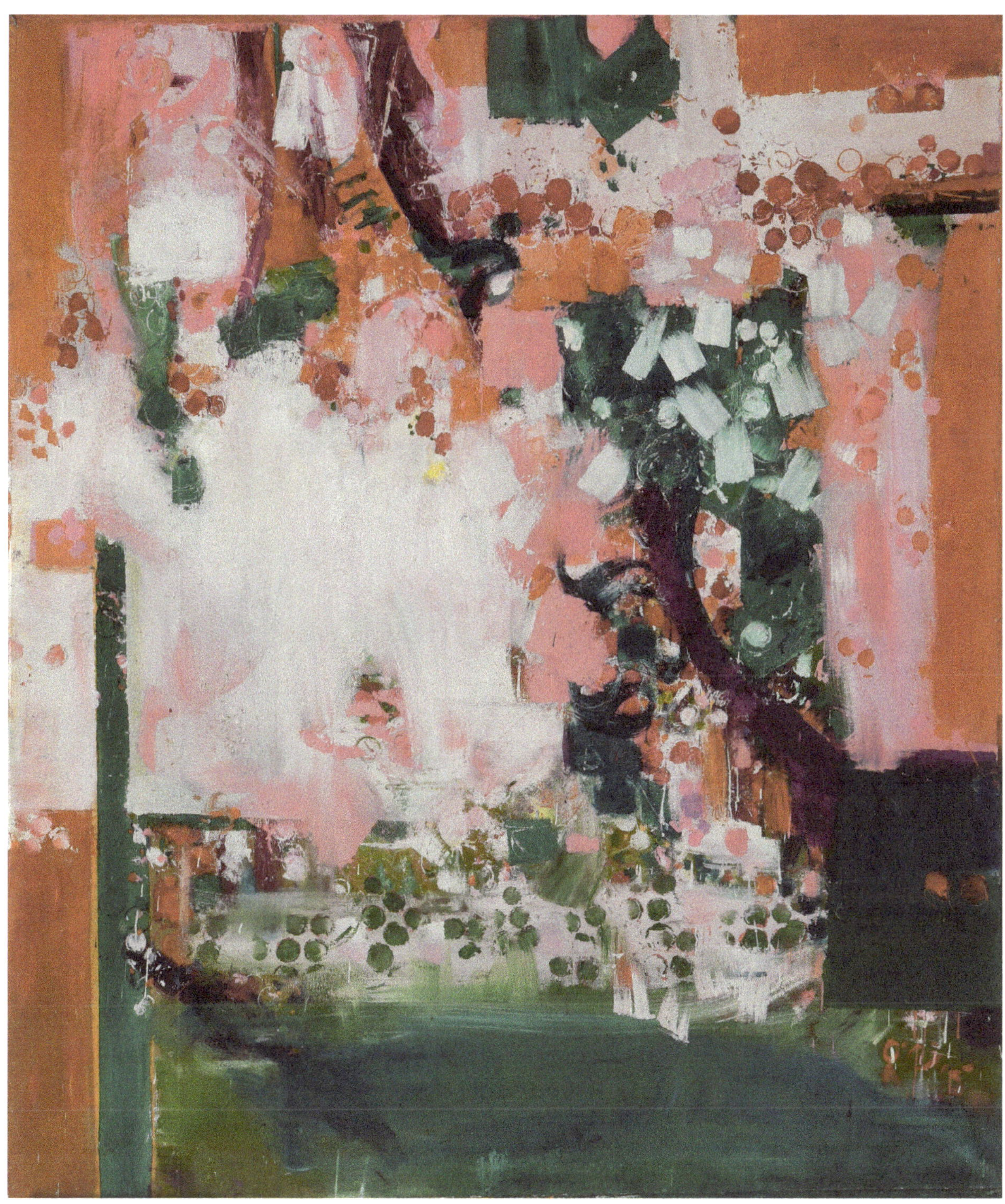

VISIONS 1974

To live given,
day and tomorrow
ignorance
not in the light, yet.

Time spent in struggle,
looking for a bright thought
to spread upon a dream
to leave traces of actions no longer vague.

Still feeling gentle touch,
a thought brought to a whole
awareness, that love is older in its wisdom
yesterdays, tomorrows, to night.

Looking out into the vast and ever moving sea,
time can devour open reality,
beyond man woman child,
leaving fear
letting waste become a tortured toy,

Those sounds of a flute sadly floating through barrier wounds
again we dare to hear, to be, again in that sea
where we began and found what has become us,

Frank O'Cain

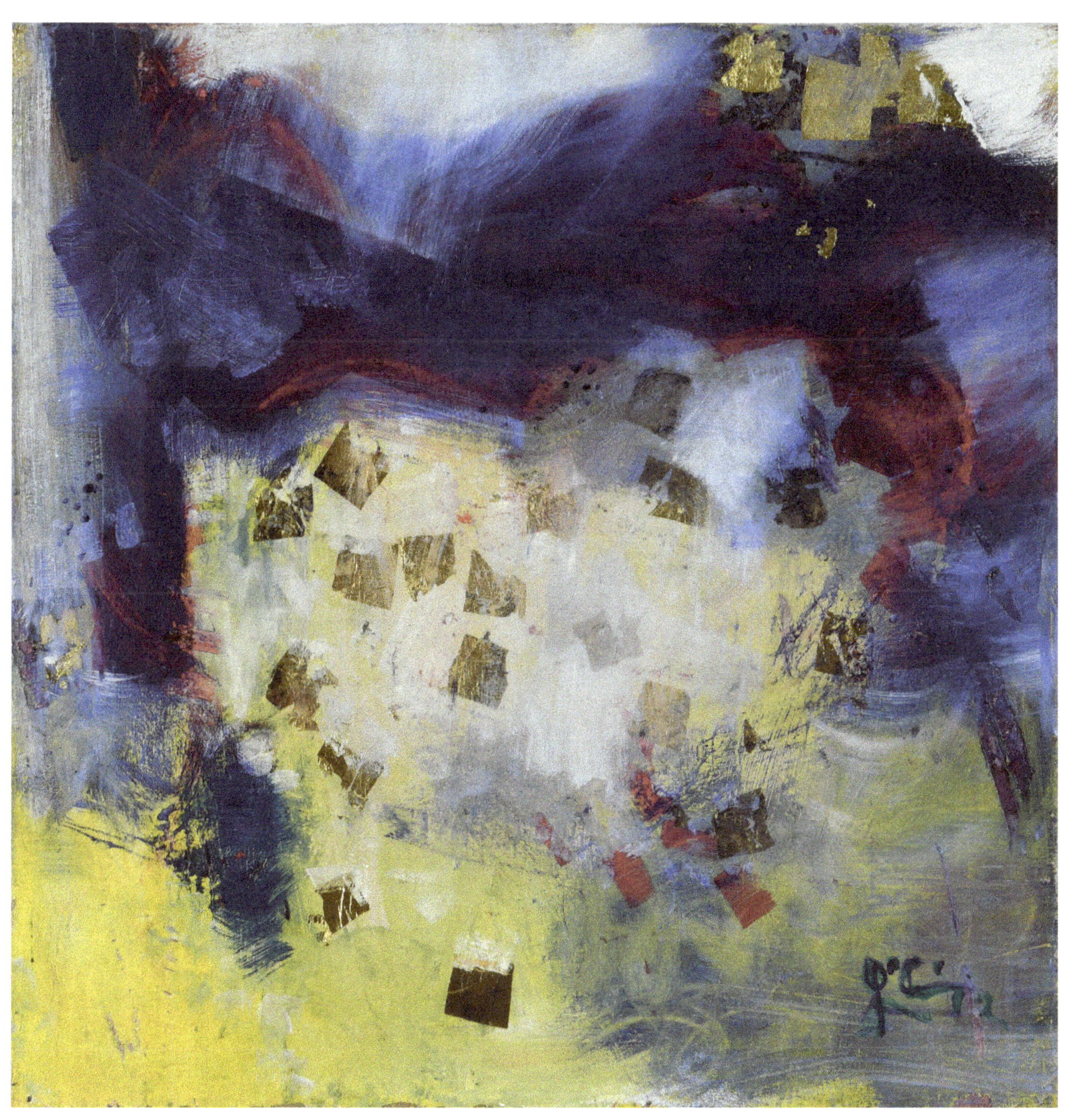

Events:
Transitions II 2012 34” x 46”

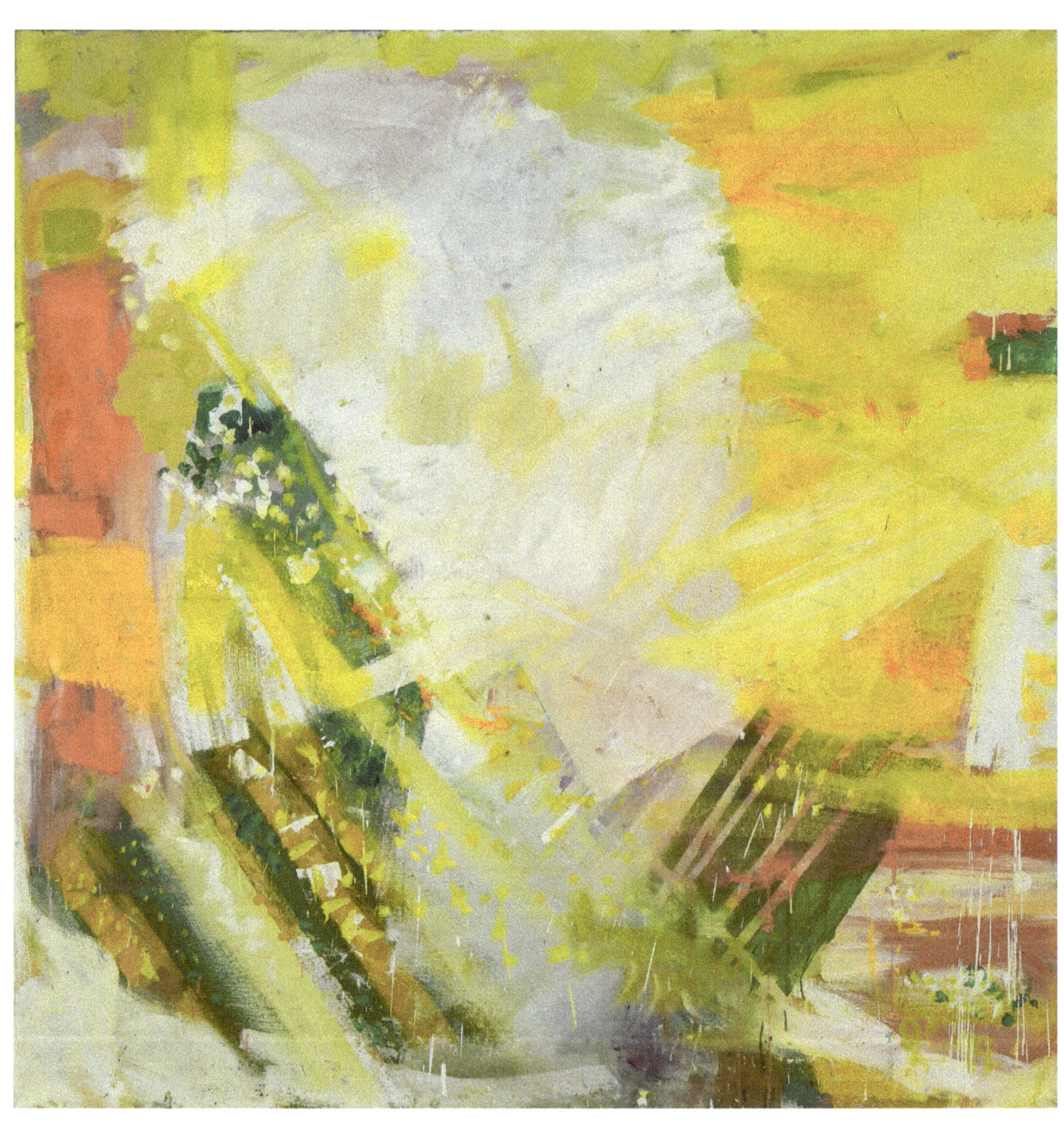

France Remembered Moving Patches	1999	64" x 65 ½"
Songs My Ancestors Sang Mating Flight	2015	38" x 56"

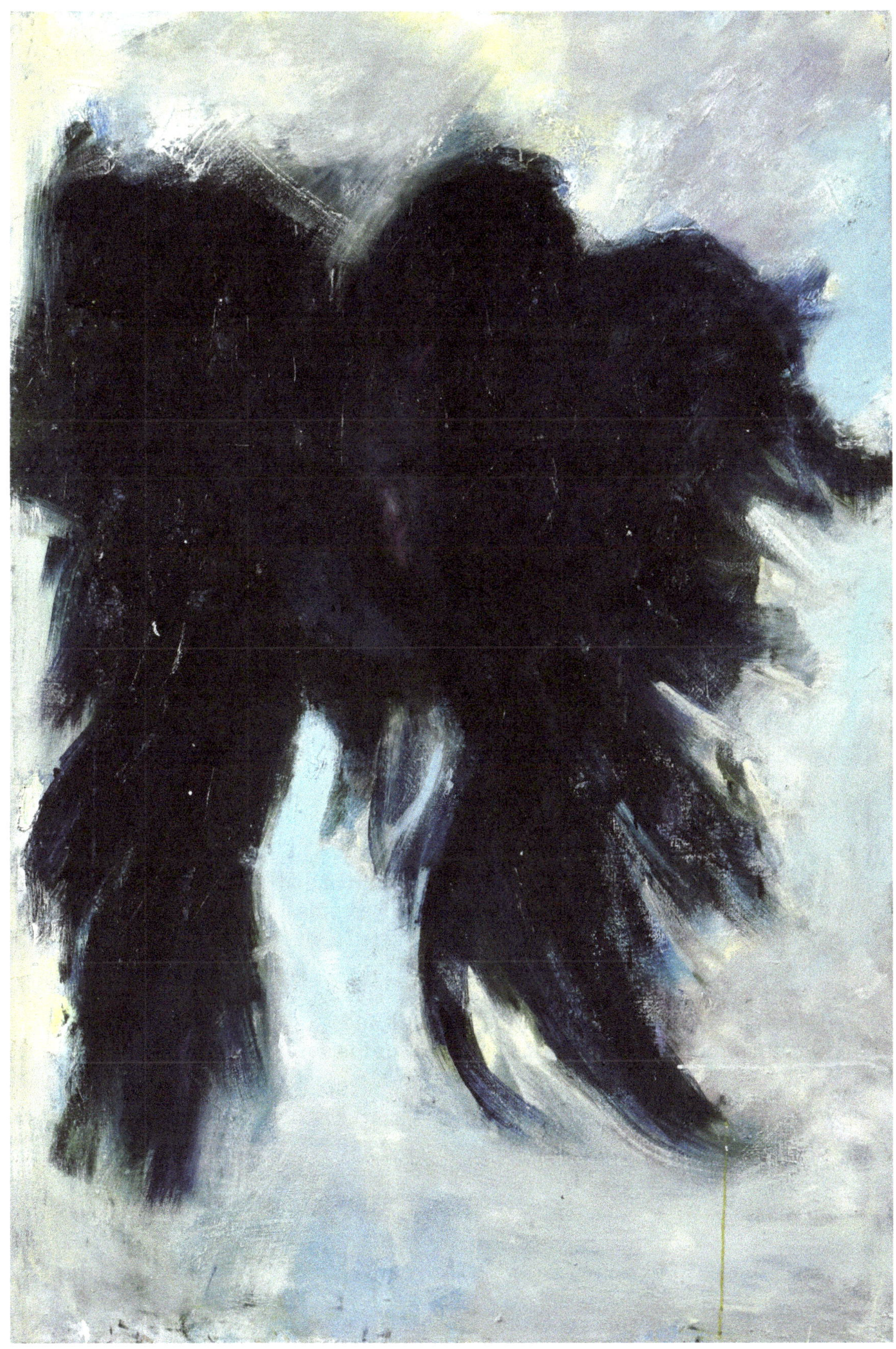

THE GATE

In the shadow beneath the sight,
murky seas wait their destiny
slowly working upon stone and metal
while voices murmur in accents from
here to every where unaware.

This one past pleasure of flesh in all
its need did bring to memory this door where
boats did come and bring to those on either side
memories of and secrets still locked in the by and by.

As midst of soft gray brings to those on either side
memories of joy and secrets still locked in the by and by.

As mist of soft gray bring quiet sunrise
the curious ponder upon this gate and
why was the time so hard upon what
once so carefully laid in gold and silver and red painted bars.

Yet the now has confused the past
with present leaving stories to be told.
Now this gate sits with the murk and growing
mold among those walls of layered color revealed
in faces of tipping walls.
Patient the sea it knows so well that it will welcome this
doorway to its endless depth.

But for now the creaking swing and stubborn rust
bear to all how strong this faith in need to overcome.
From sunrise to sunset past to present lingered giving
to eyes of need their resolution.

While the all in all comes and goes the dark and
waiting gate creaks and groans as in wait for the next to being to toil.

Frank O'Cain

Whispers Through Time;
The Gate 2009 30" x 58"

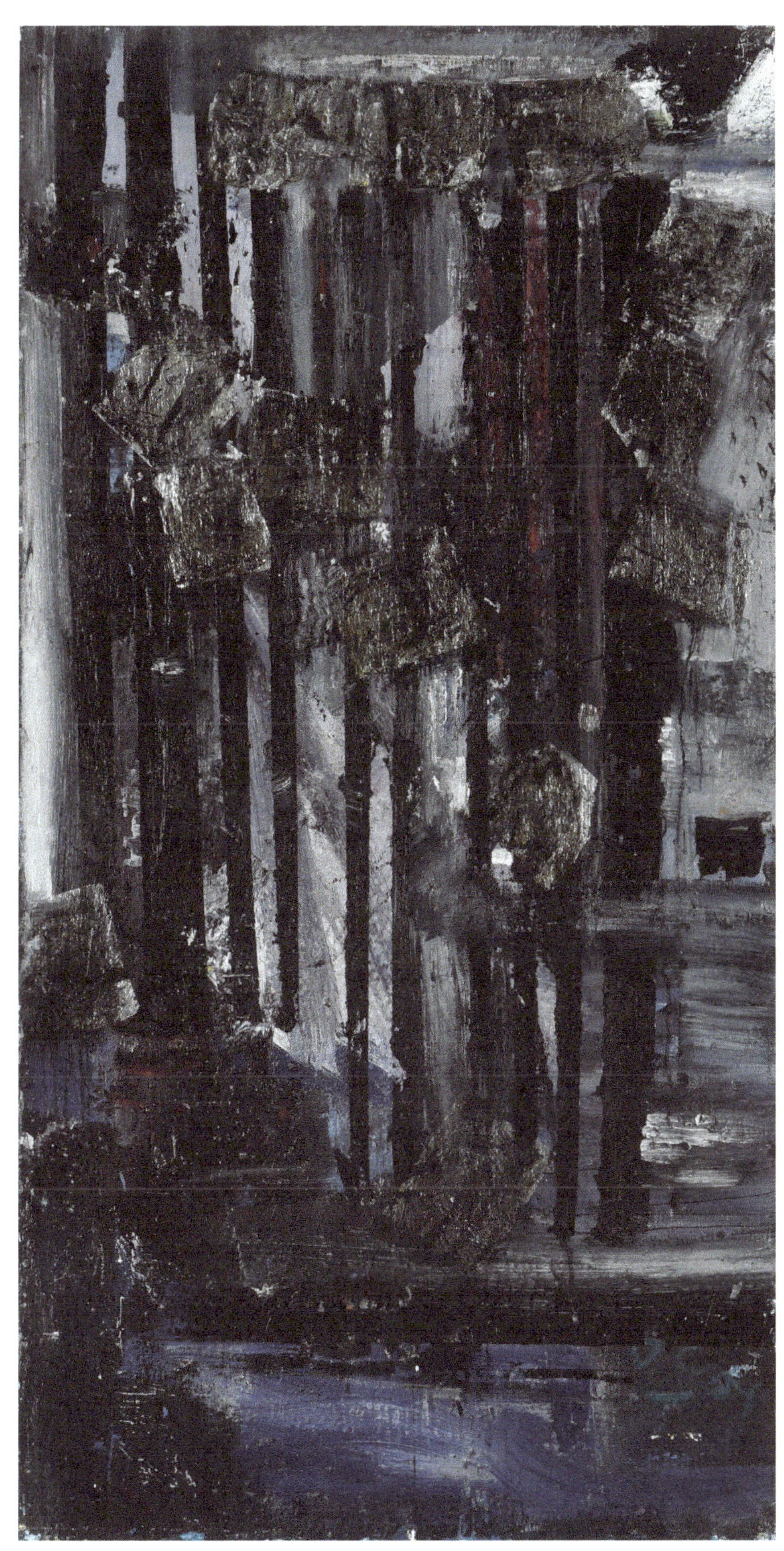

Embrace

As colors moved from action
to subdued

A white mass floated upon
the oranges, reds, and greens

Giving us a moment to feel
all that would become

Spring's Winter
Opus III 2018 48" x 36"

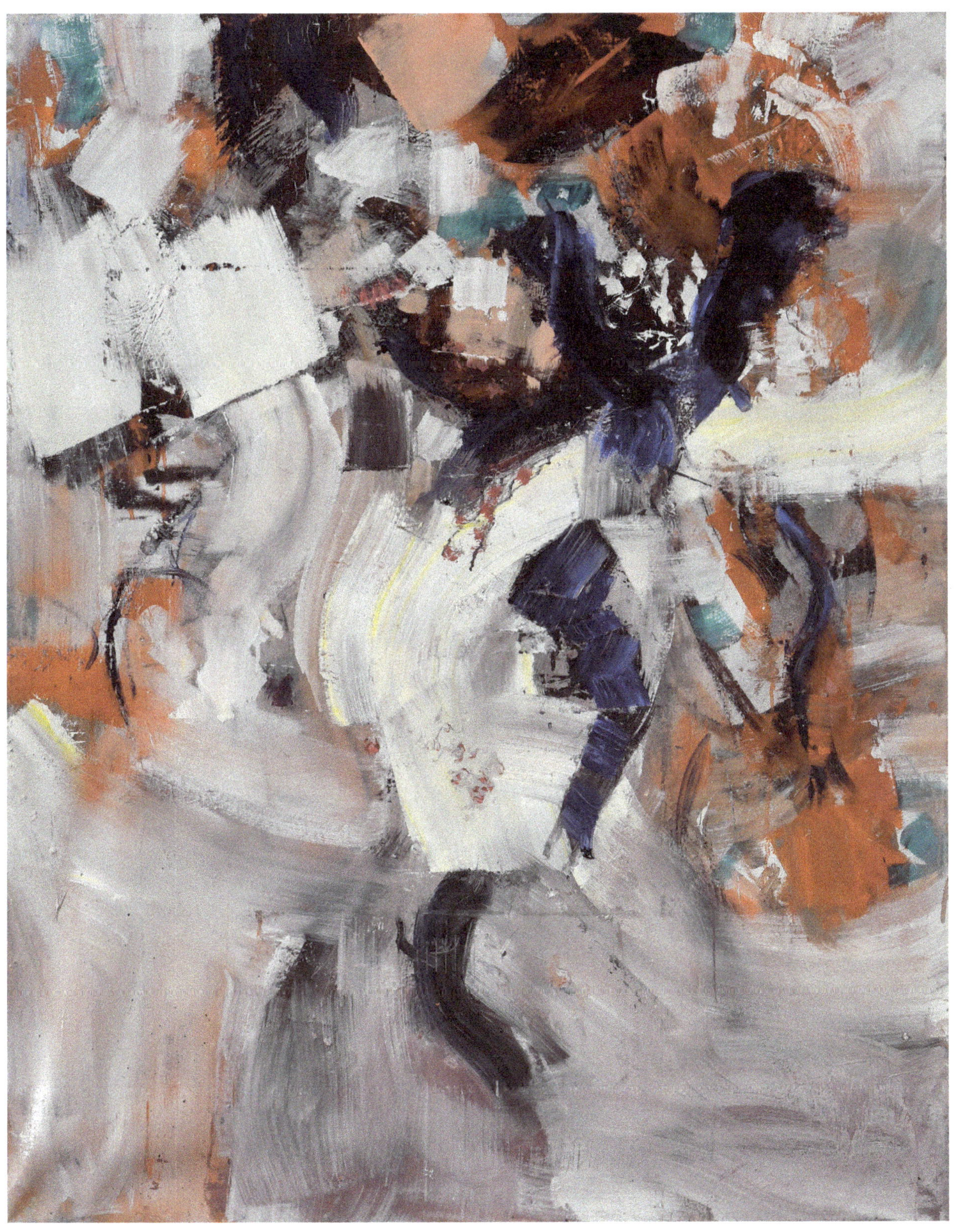

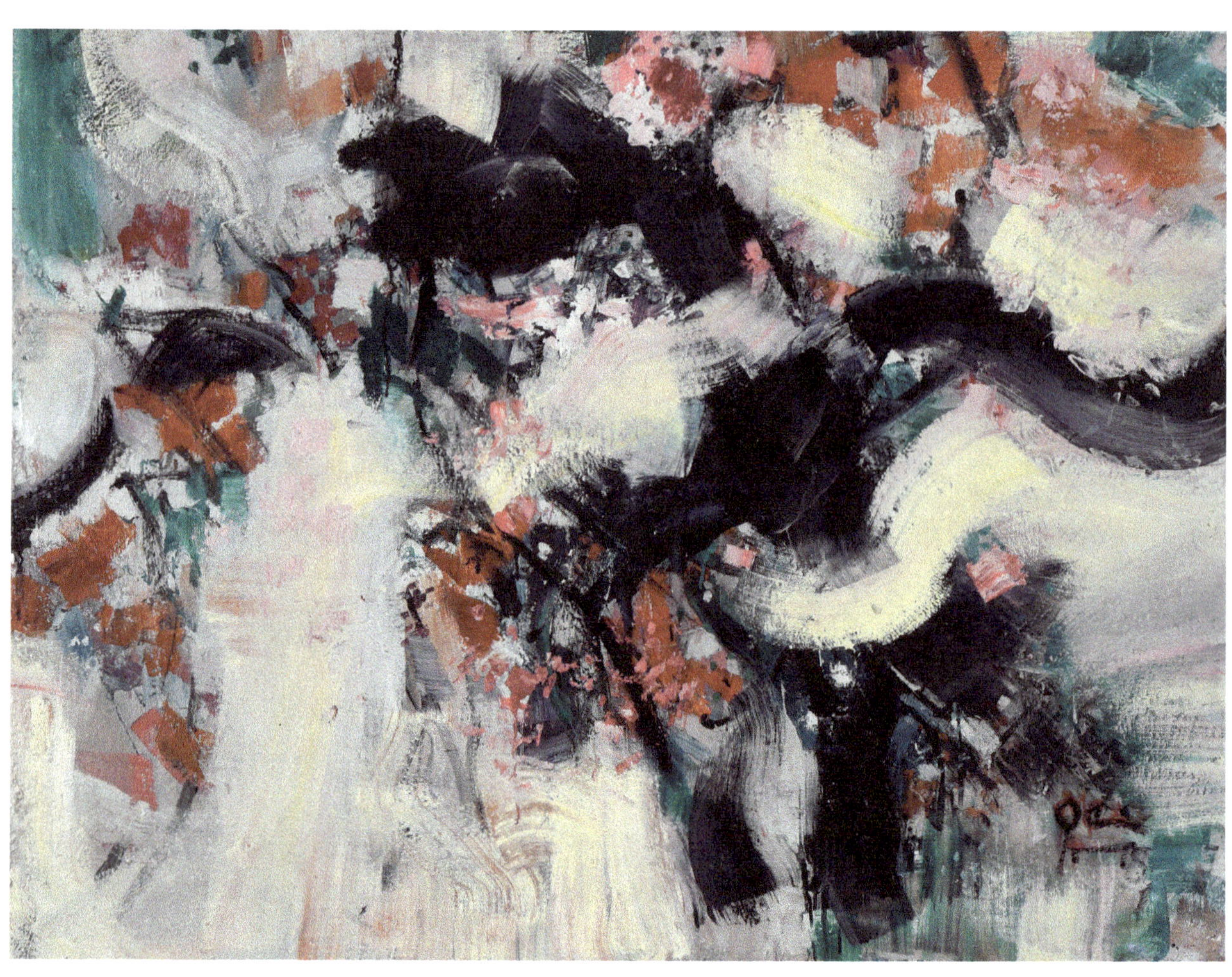

"Spring's Winter Opus VII	2018	30" x 30"
Songs My Ancestors Sang Land Rhythm panels	2018	50" x 60" two

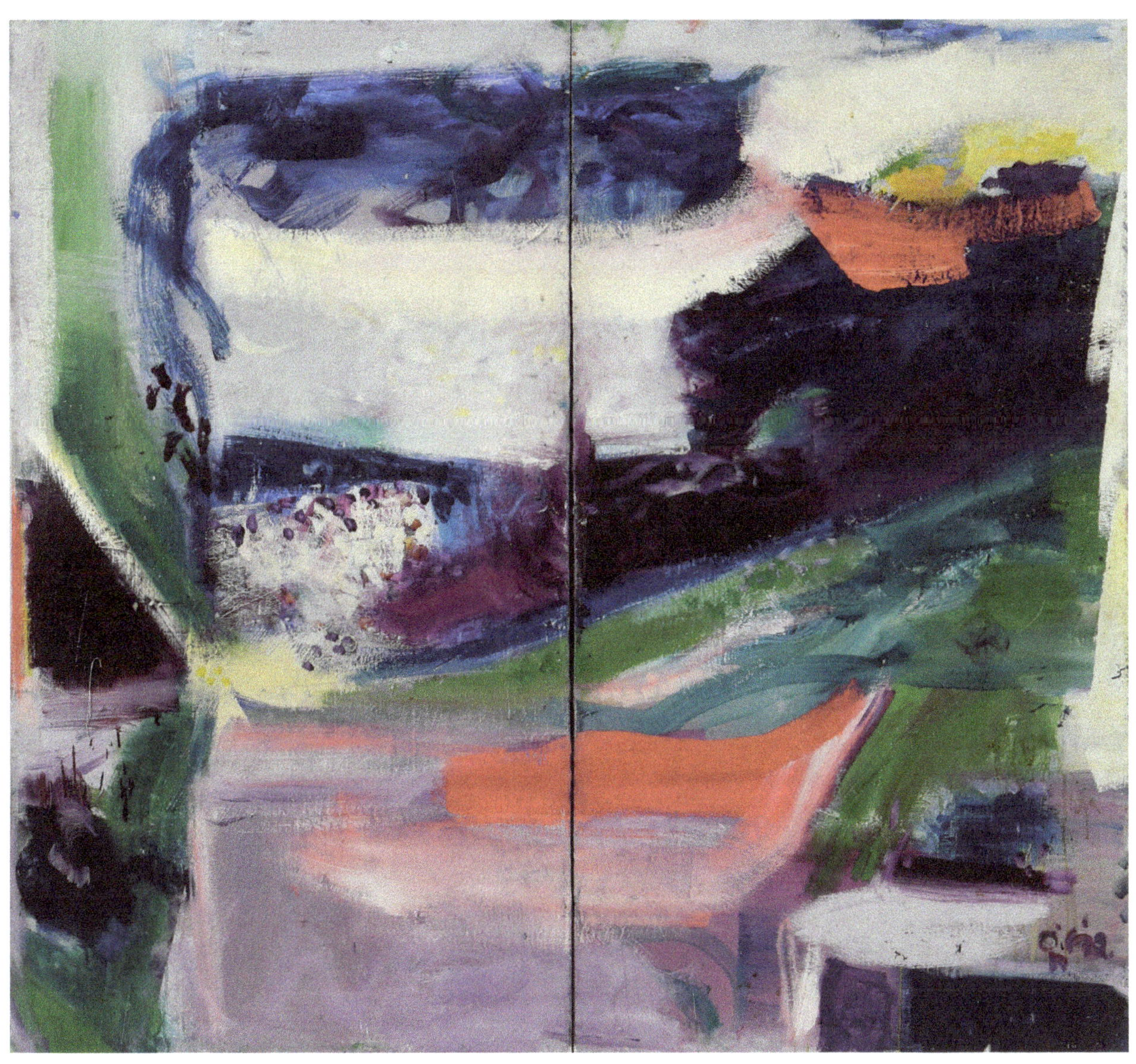

Sitting on the edge of history

By the water

Echo of water on the canvas – Staffa

Two crows flying

Birds in flight

Cave painting deep beneath

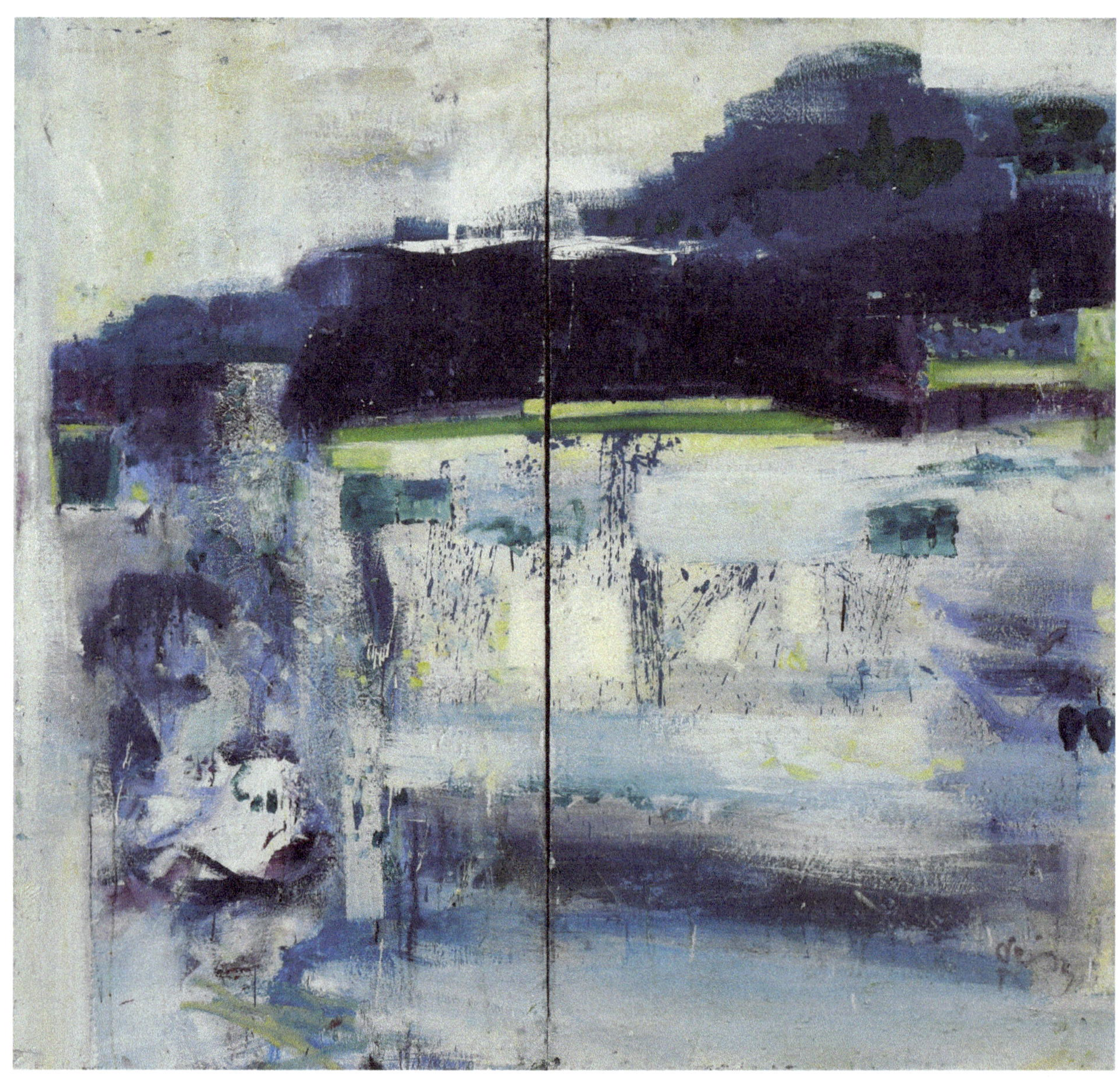

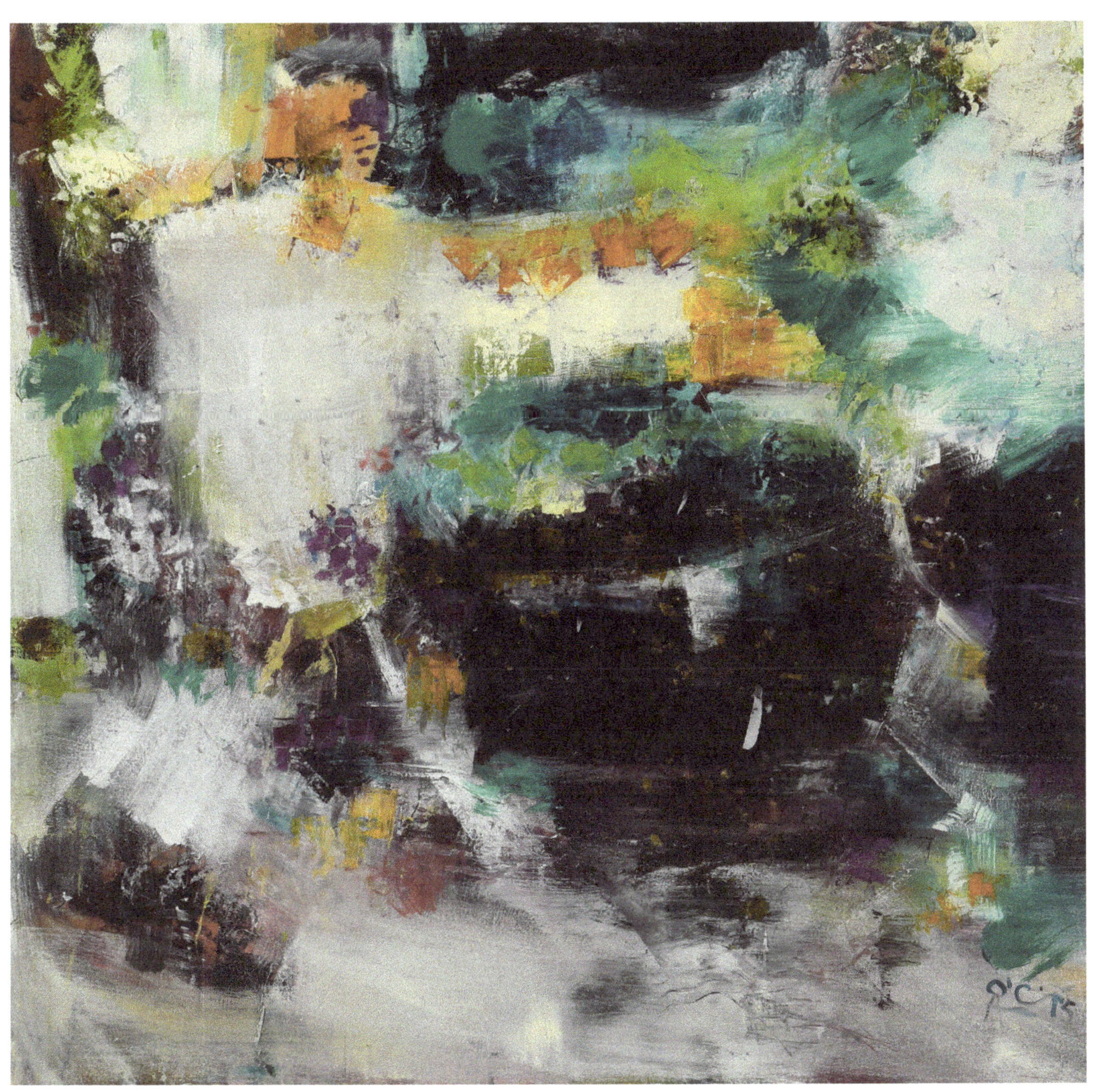

Songs My Ancestors Sang Remembered Actions	1975	36" x 49" each
Songs My Ancestors Sang Opus I, Secrets	2015	50" x 48"

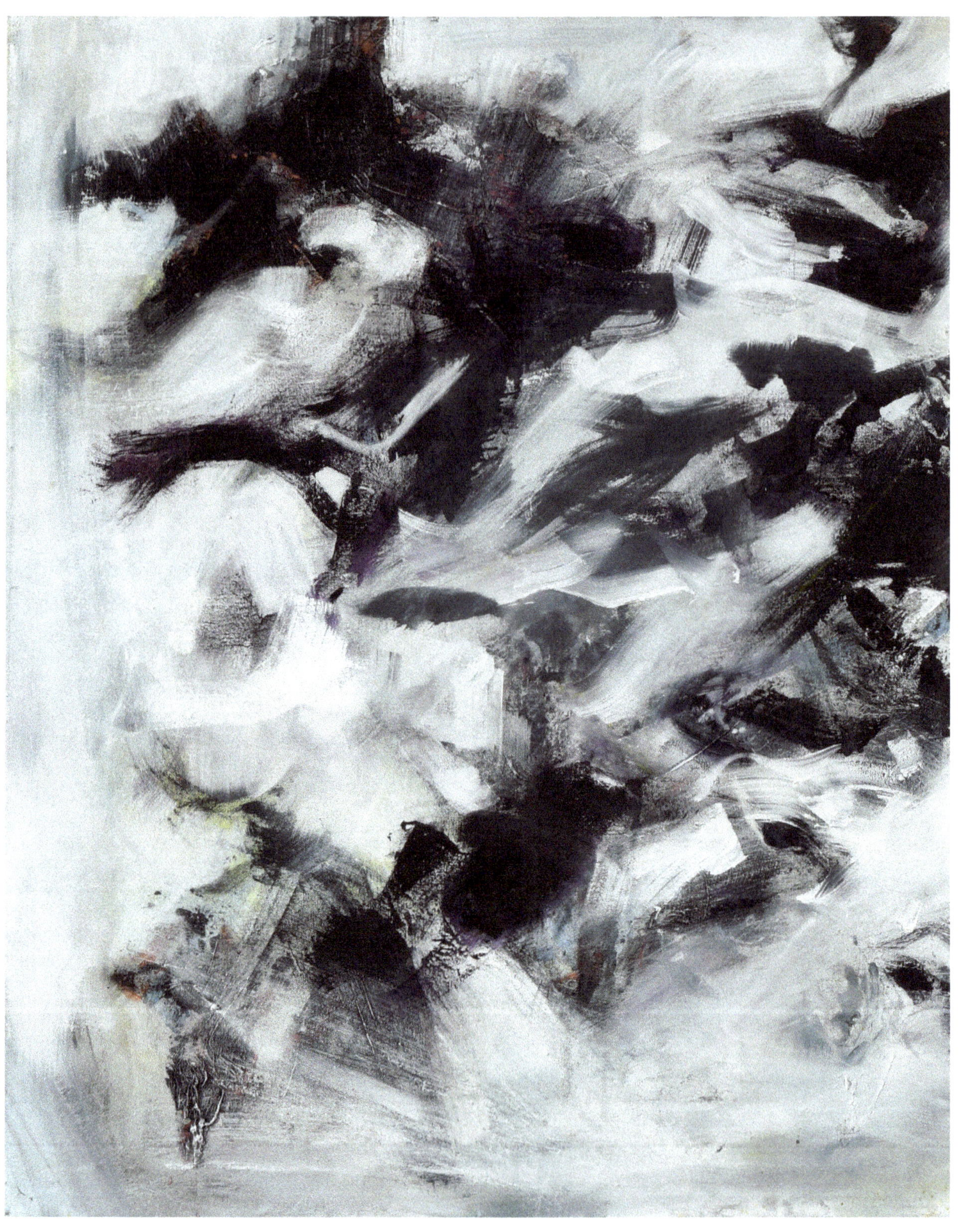

Songs My Ancestors Sang
The Screaming Flight 2018 72" x 44"

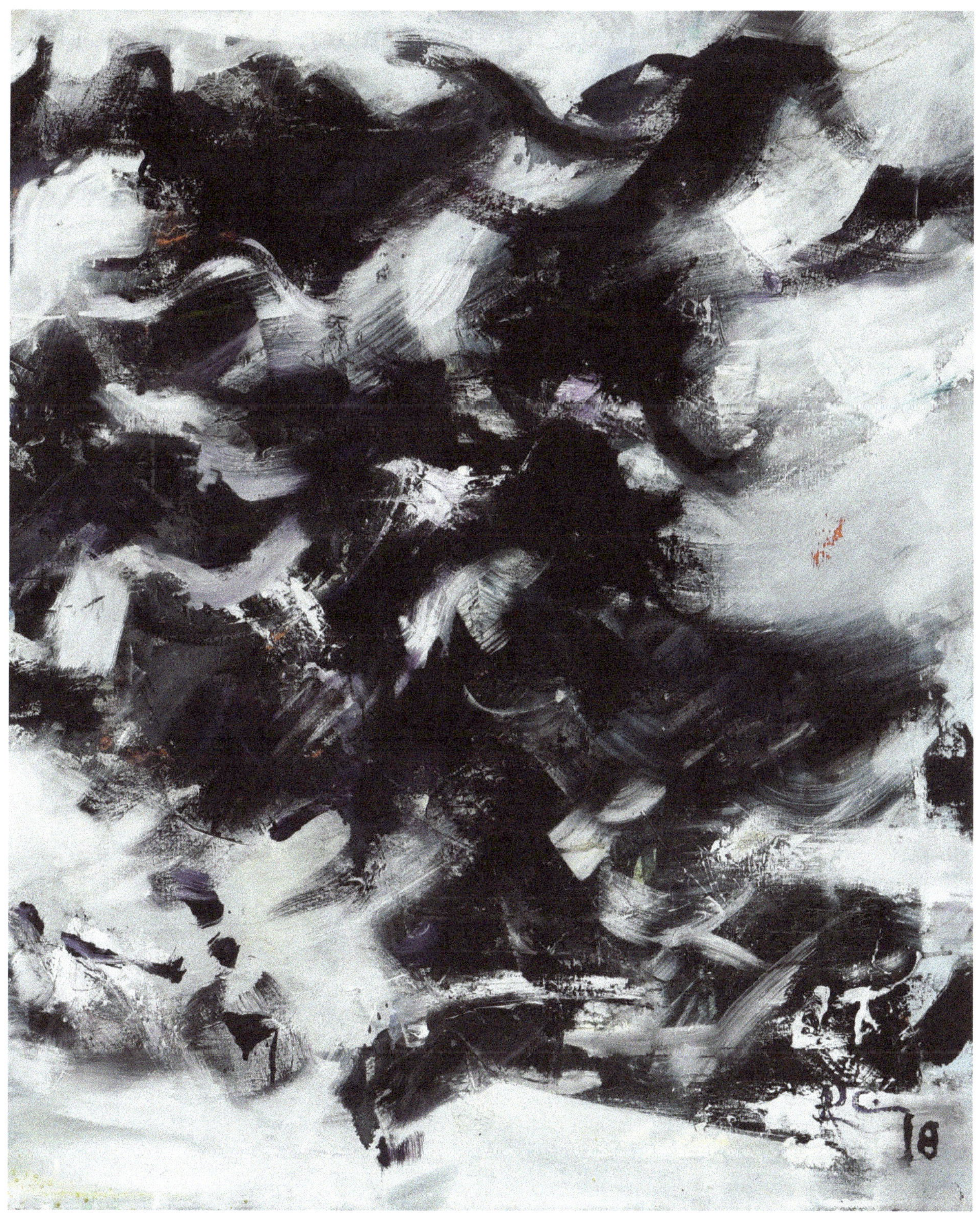

Surprise winter storm in the middle of spring

Sudden change in light and color

Dream sequence

Flecks of light bouncing in nature

Winter came back and covered it

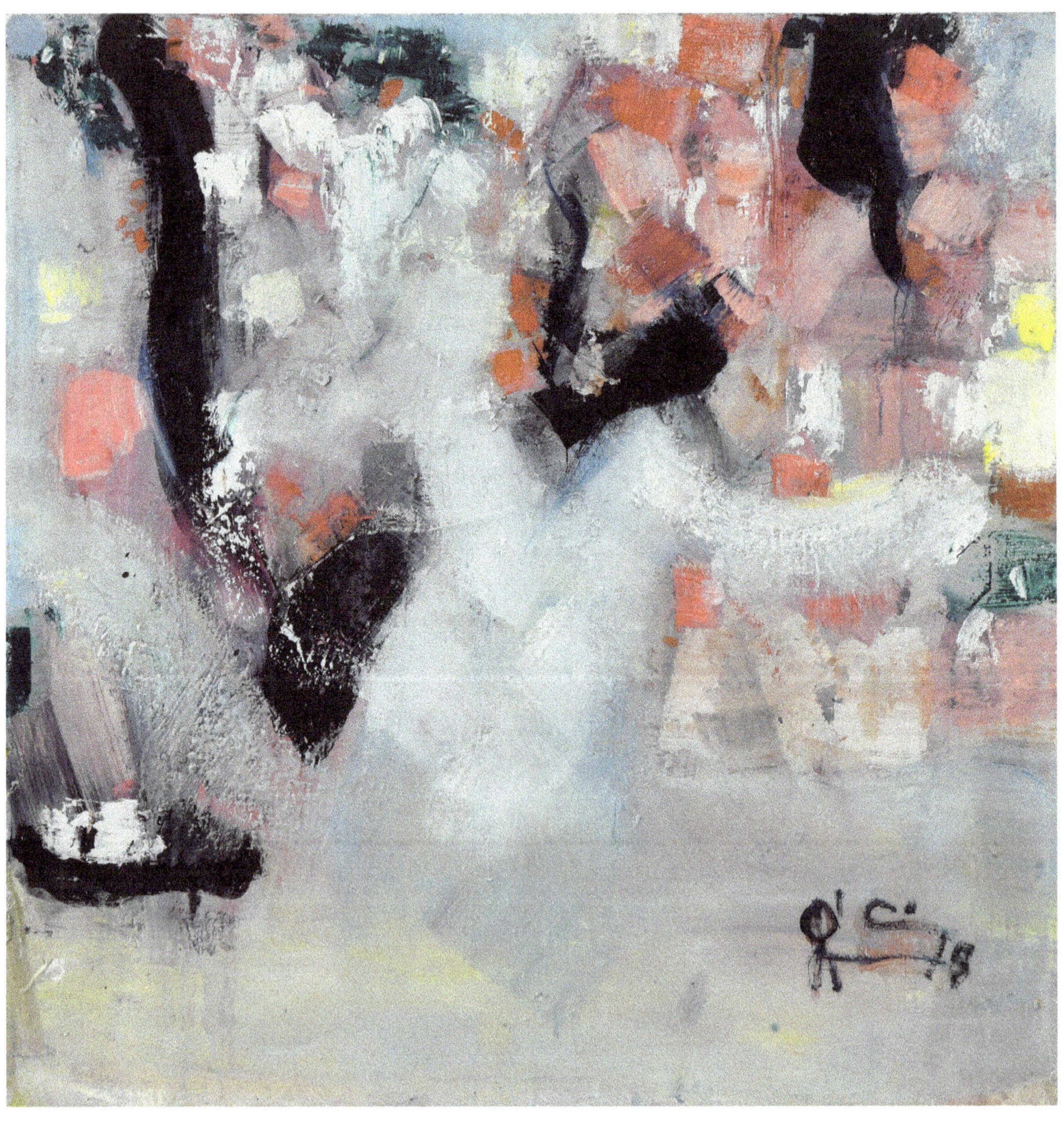

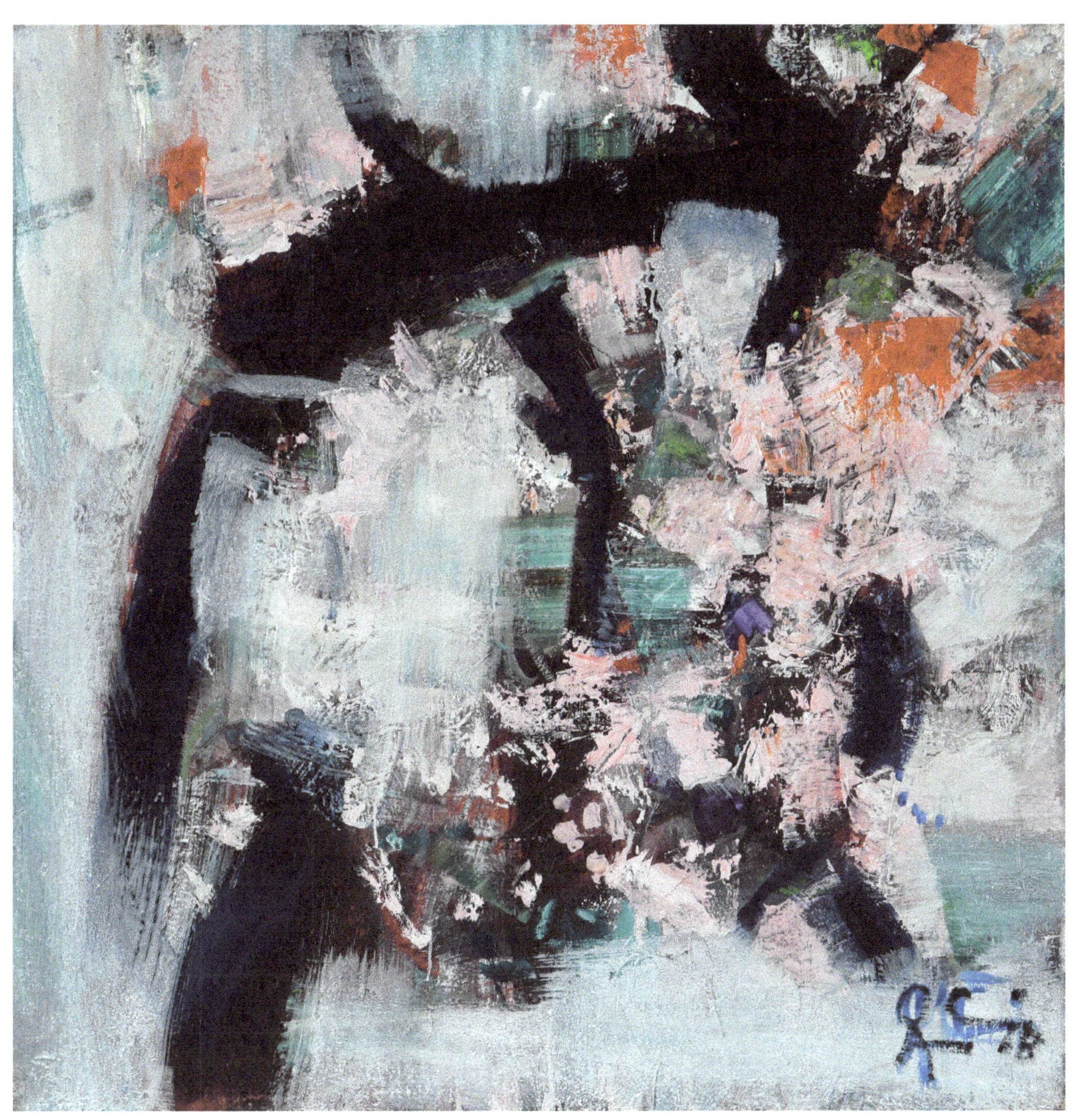

Spring's Winter Opus II	2018	30" x 30""
Spring's Winter Opus IV	2018	30" x 30""

The missing elements of the ancient: rich with association

The energy of belief let loose with finding a different idea

The energy moving up and away

Watching the land in ancient time

Moving history

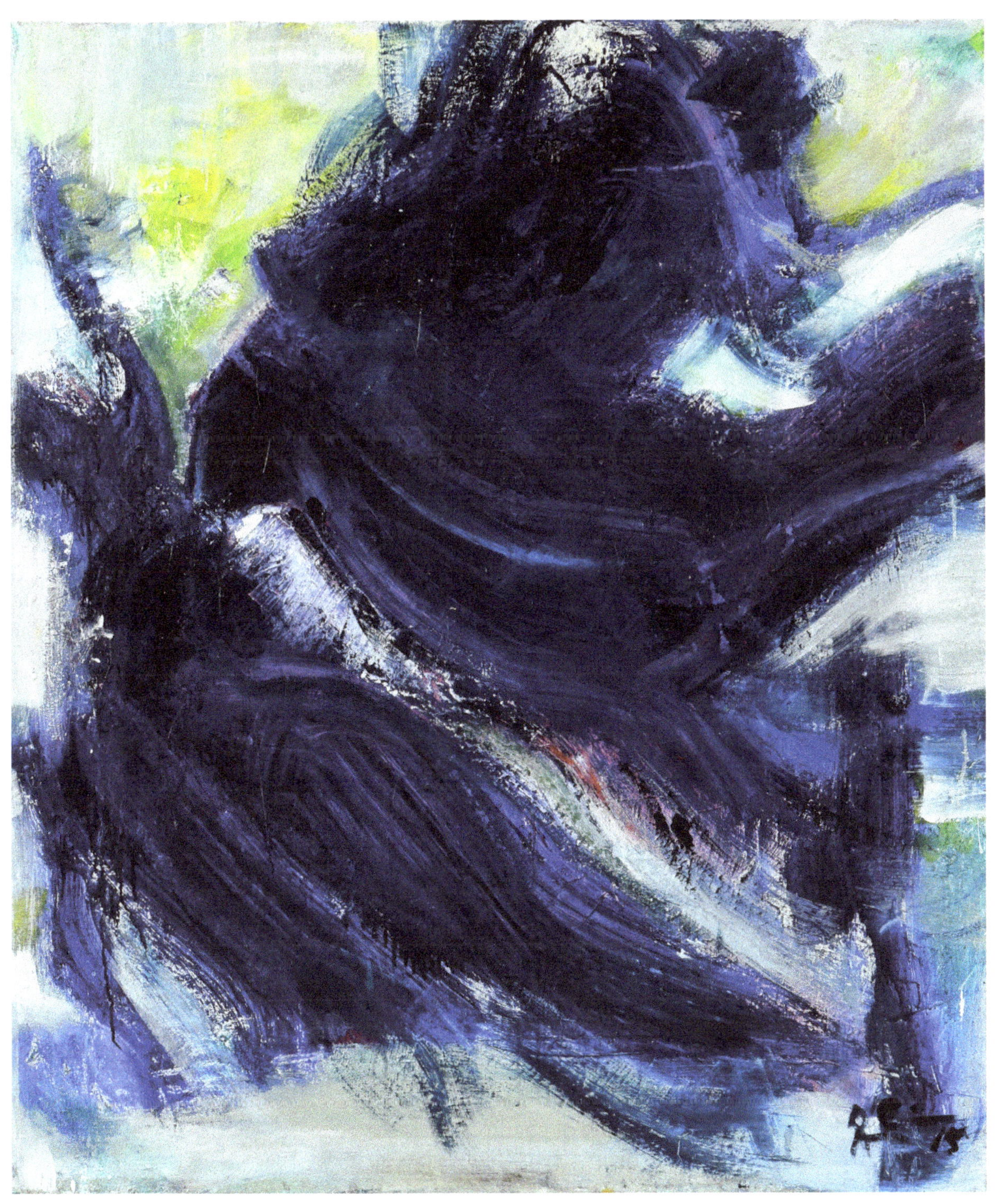

Songs My Ancestors Sang
Dispute 2018 40" x 56"

FINDING THE PATH

The manifestation so dark
    so still
    so quiet
    in the watching
    the waiting
We live in the energy of each other
    the long stories, the endless complaints
    They are the stealers of souls
    the consumers of strength
The tales of after battles and the swarm that comes
    and takes away pieces
    of
    fallen worriers
    before we gather the power for our next battle.
The stories, so long ago.
    Now
    the seeds yet to rest in the soul
    become the feast for the hopping dark searchers,
    finding their tomorrow
Still
    there are the ones that come to see
    to leave a gift of some shiny bubble
    and watch for the reward expecting to appear
And
    some stay and play
    and give warning when strangers are about
Always for the ones that become their mates
    there is the mystery
    the laugh, you can not hear
    the quiet being so deep inside
    they are play that lives in moments far from worlds
    we know
The stories come and give us a memory of life rich in sharing
    for now the time to watch to wait
    to fill the spirit with gifts
All all the gifts now here,
    in every line or shade of dark
    this is the place my hand does stroke
    does leap into the dance of life and
    whirl about the blessing.
Thankful
    for the long path and all it provides.

Frank O'Cain

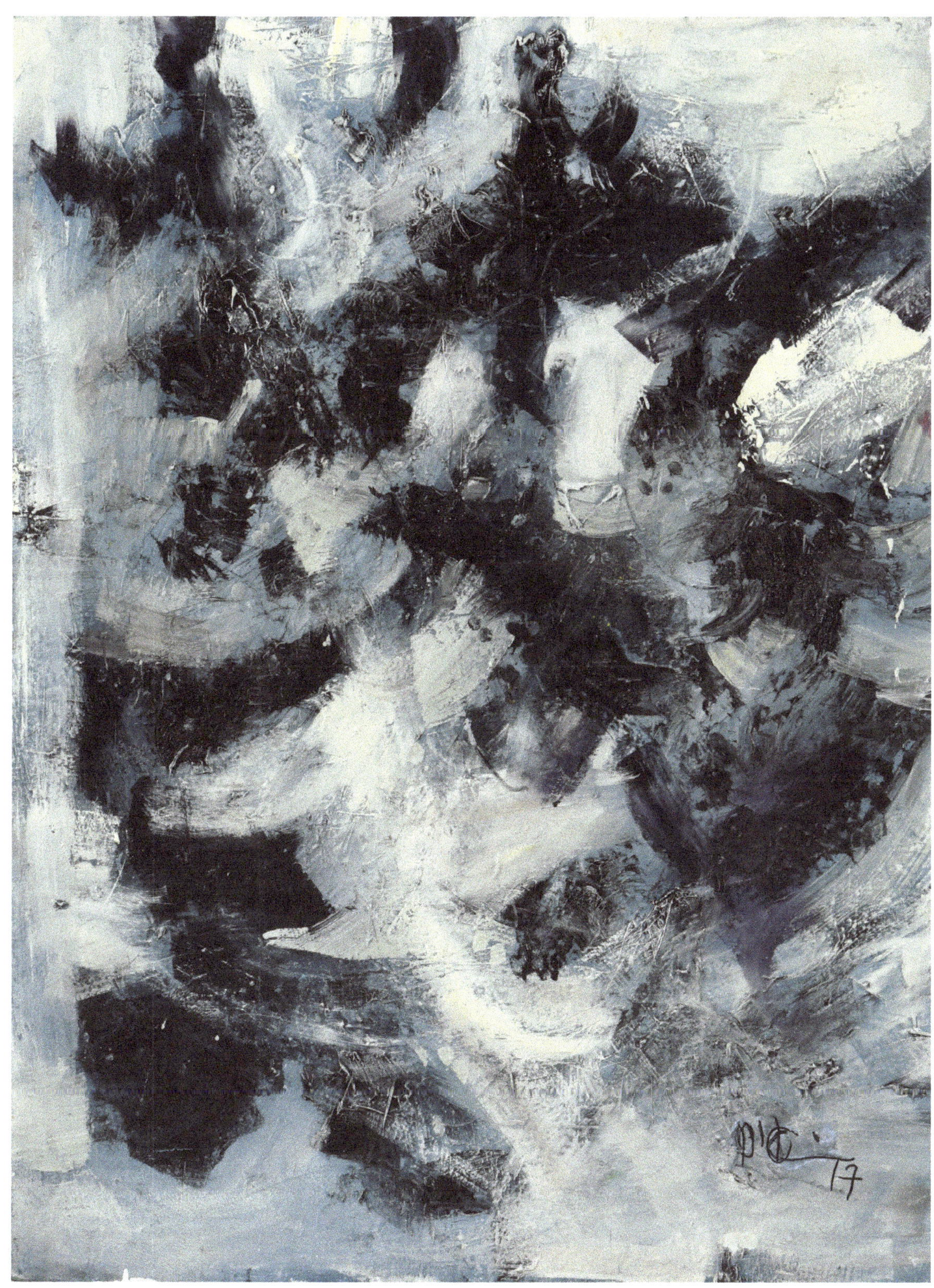

Songs My Ancestors Sang
Shapes in Flight 2015 44" x 50"

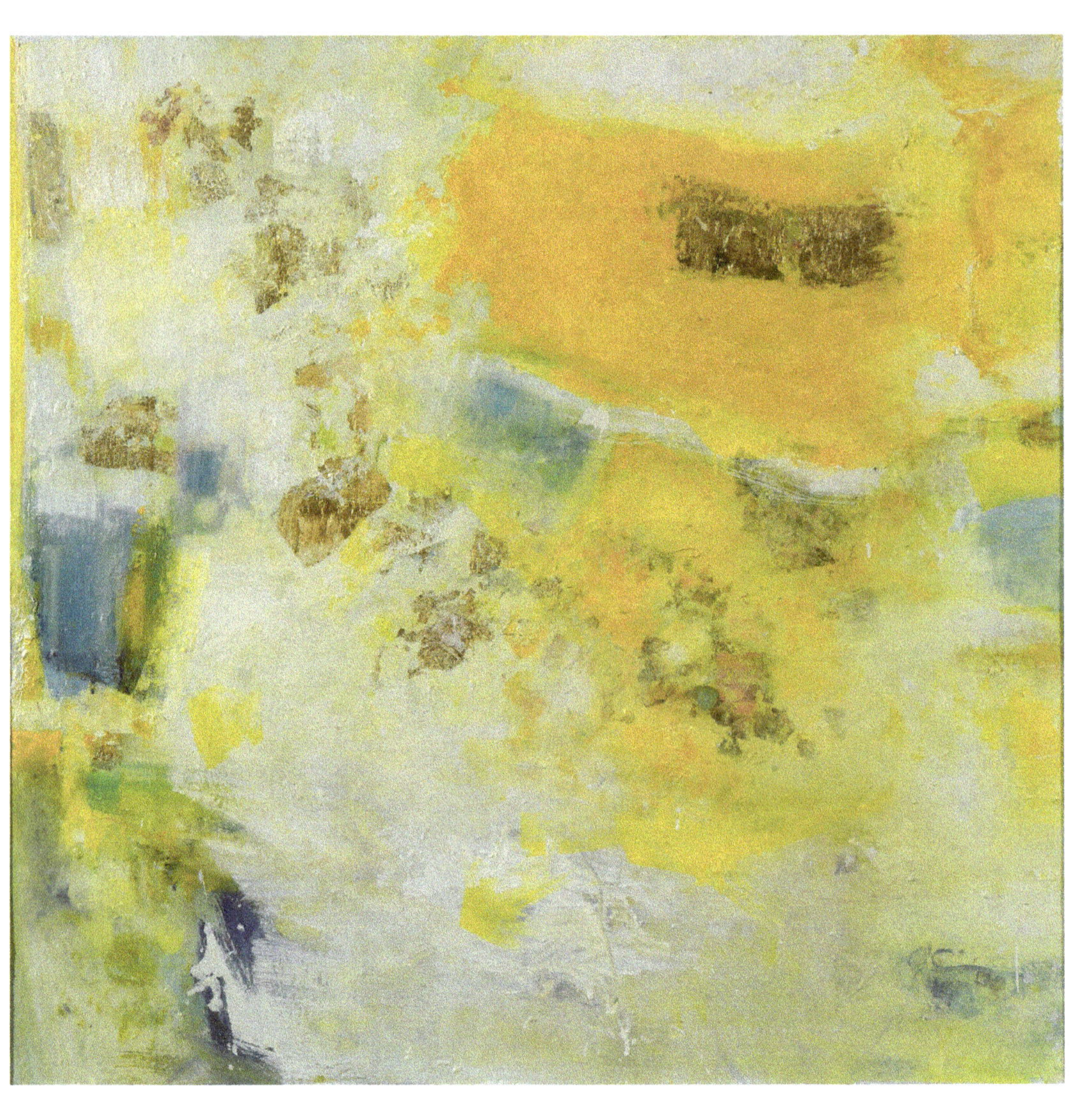

France Remembered Sensations	2005	64" x 55"
Homage to Heildegard	2018	64" x 72"

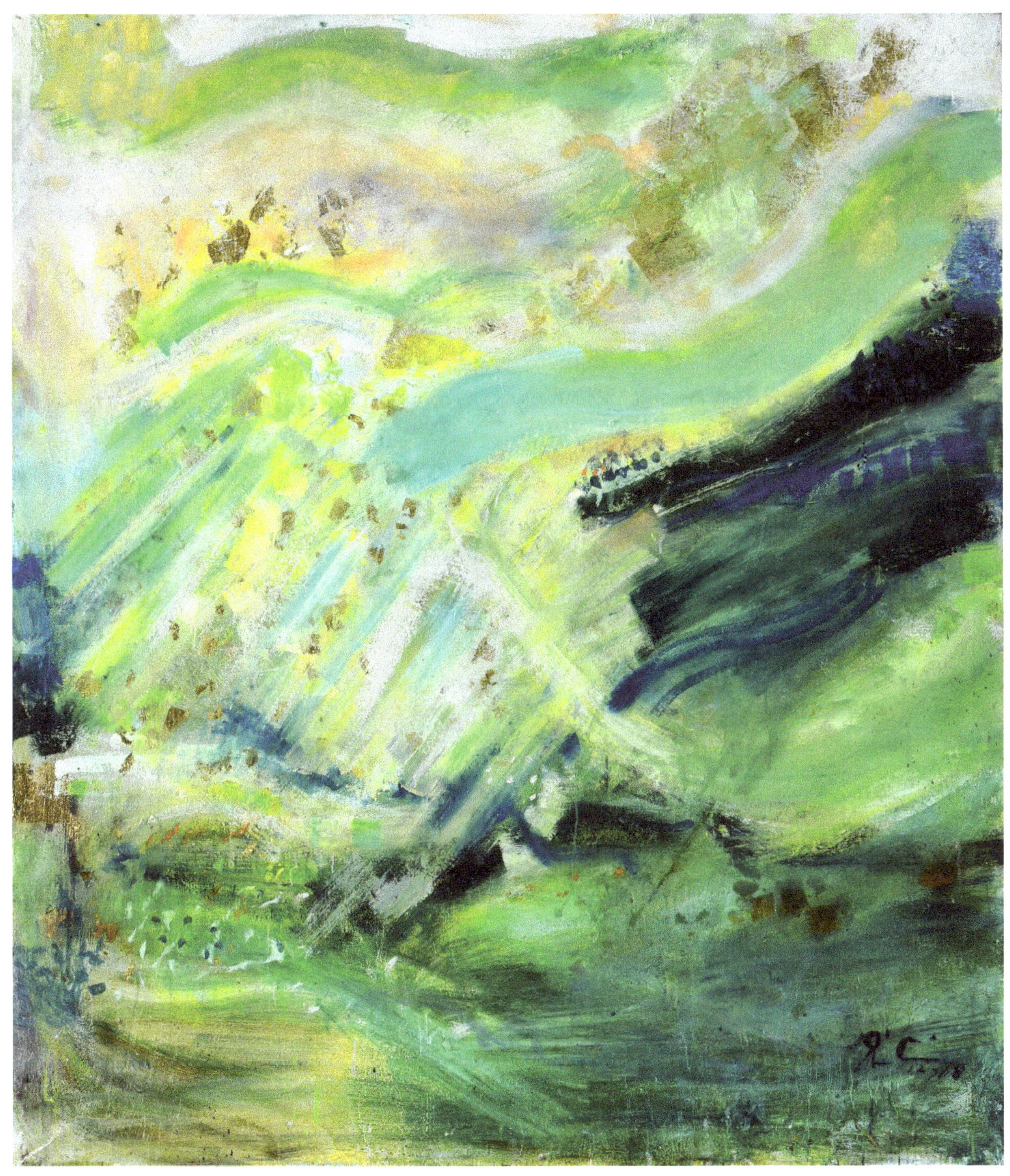

PLAY

In fields of long limbs,
we so wanted to reach when we where six.

Silent as words fall,
from a obvious mind
laugh at the waste in sounds living in there scraping motion
ignorance how it feeds hate,
and turn room life
knowing that sleep will fill the night in dreams
that will become a new reality
so
sleep in tender thought
while the beast struggle

Not a whisper
can extract the life that is now in sleep
till seven comes
and once again embraces life

Frank O'Cain

Songs My Ancestors Sang
Broken Altar 2001 51" x 51"

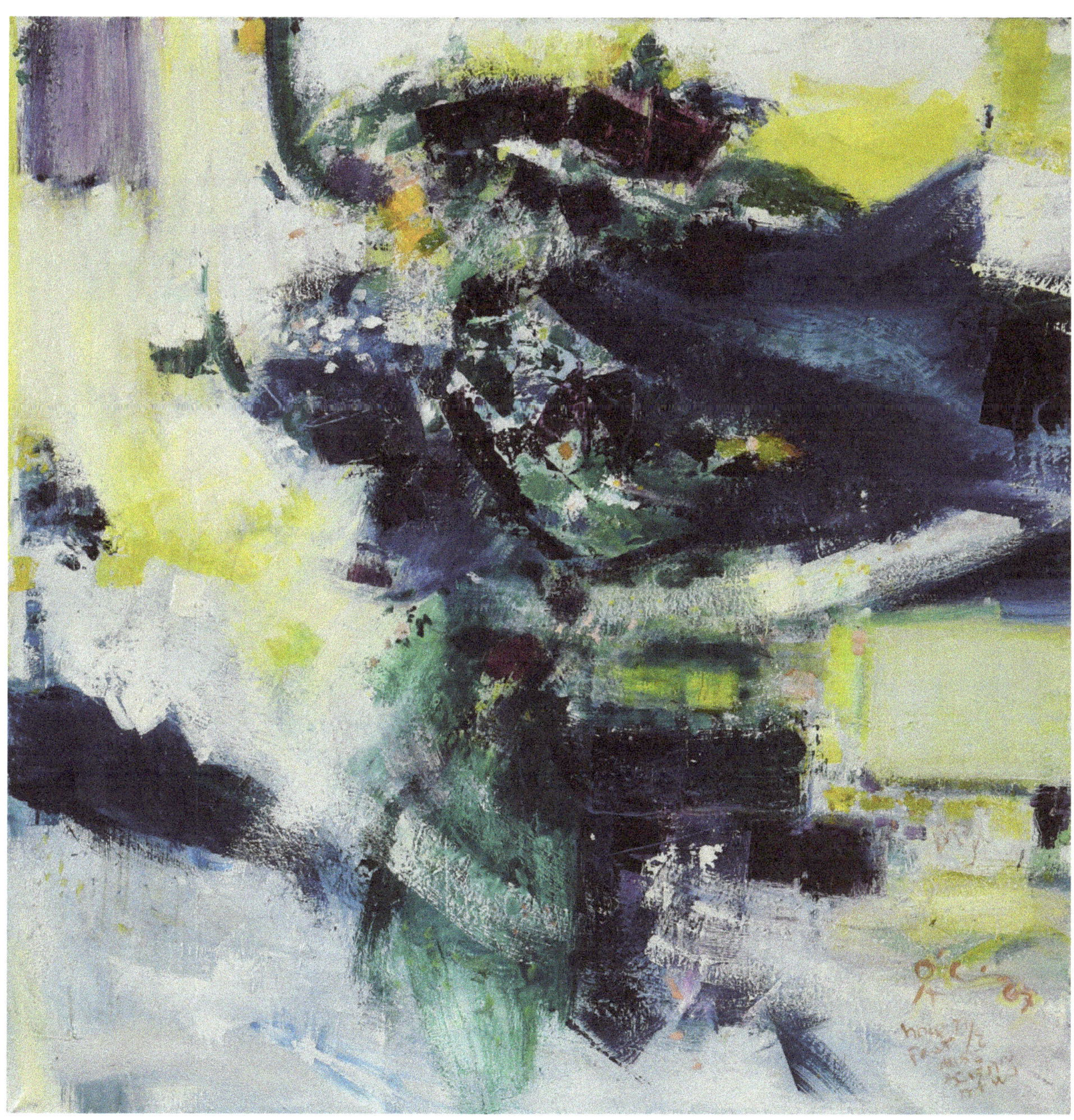

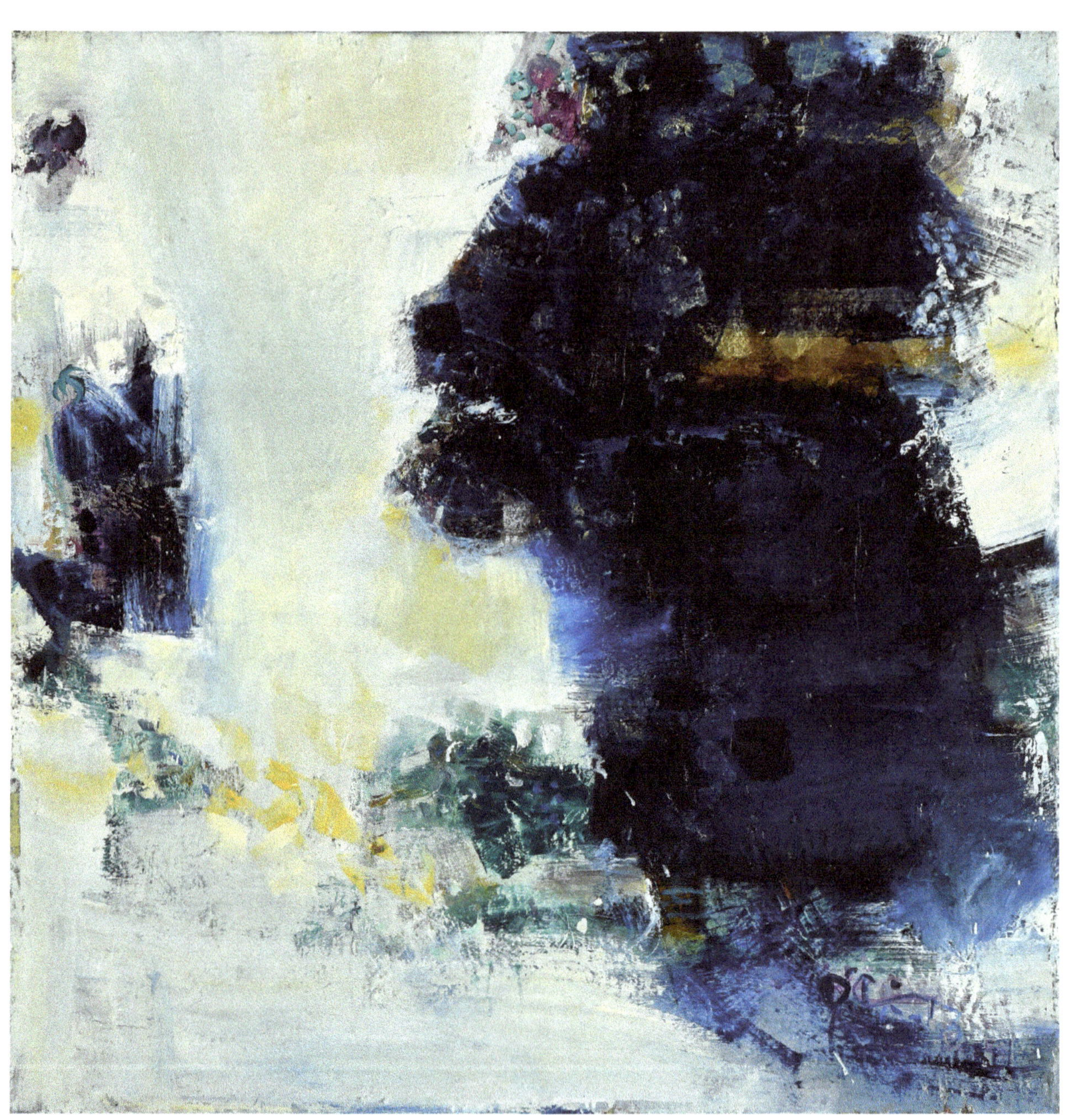

Songs My Ancestors Sang		
Coming Upon Shapes II	2018	38” x 40”
Events:		
Effects of Wind in Soft Sound	2010	70” x 70”

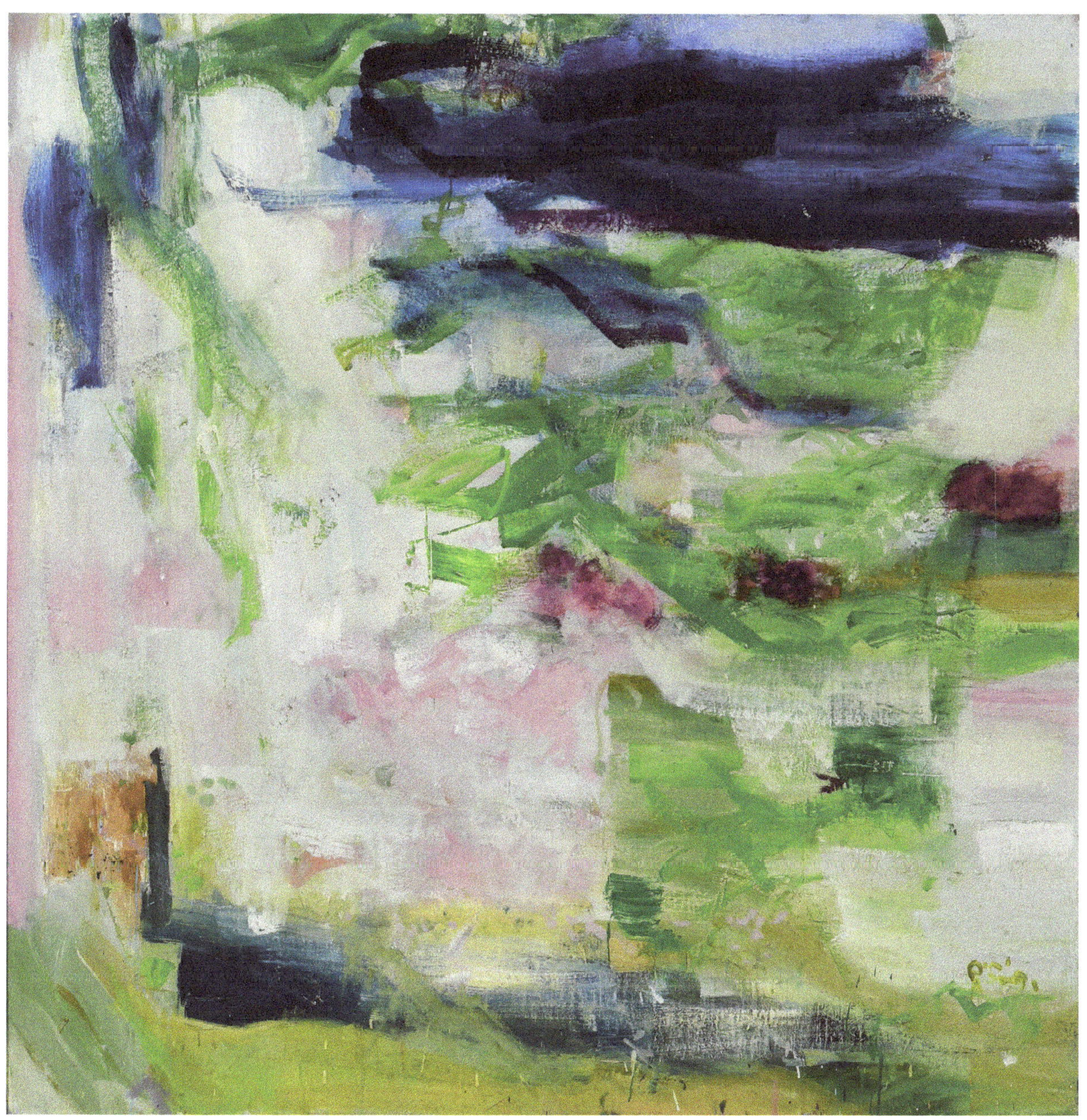

MEMORIES

As the now older
remains lay in a
screaming madness the
mind within slid into
the beginning.
The eyes no longer
saw the group standing
about him waiting for
the pain to subside the
drugs to do what they
are meant to; instead
of directing his anger at
those in waiting he was
now in the covered
wagon of his birth
listening and watching
his entrance.
The pain of the
woman giving into the
enviable struggled with
the stubbornness of
the soul trying to def
the gray place it was
about to enter.
A soiled cloth clamped
between tight jaw
holding back scream of
pure agony. The
young girls constant cry
of "Push! Push! Hit
upon the dim sounds
that were coming through
the cloth and the biting
pain as child to be
slowly emerged from
its place of quiet to the
now arriving doctor
that took the place to
receive and hold the
new born up for
inspection. Short the
stay the doctor wrote
in the Bible, baby born.

Frank O'Cain

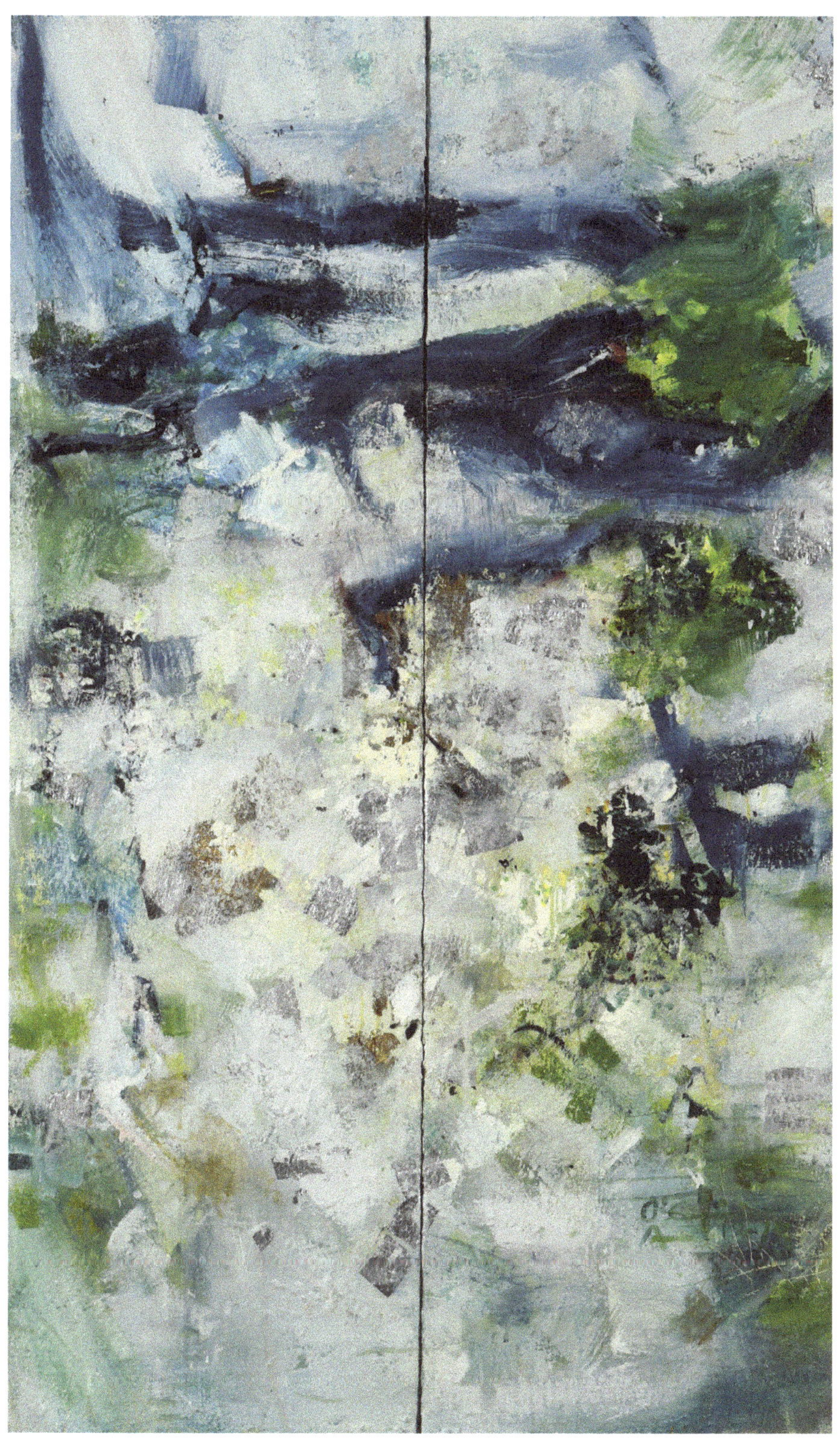

Study for Effects of the Wind II 2014 36 1/2 x 72”
two panels

Frank O'Cain was born in San Diego, California. He has been an instructor at the Art Students League of New York for almost thirty years imparting an approach to abstract art that started with Cezanne, was interpreted by Hans Hofmann, and was taught to Frank O'Cain and others at the League by Vaclav Vytlacil. He is also unique in that his abstract art also derives from an elaborate study of long-forgotten fifteenth-century techniques. For a time, Mr. O'Cain's oil paintings involved no fewer than a hundred separate glazes. Recently, he has been exploring a new approach to space in painting. As he says, "I am always wandering about in the unknown, asking myself questions, creating new problems, finding fresh possibilities."

Mr. O'Cain has had one-man shows at Purdue University; the Miriam Perlman Gallery, Chicago, 1981; the Miriam Perlman Gallery, Flint, Michigan; the Princeton Art Association; Levitan Gallery I and II, New York City, 1969, 1977; the Saginaw Art Museum; the Ella Sharp Museum, Jackson, Mississippi; Northern Illinois University; the Theano Stahelin Kunstsalon, Zurich, Switzerland; and at the Elizabeth V. Sullivan Gallery (at the League Residency at Vyt, 2013). He has participated in group shows at DD&B Gallery, New York City, 1996, 1998; Gallery Korea, New York City, 1999; Gen Paul Gallery, Paris, France, 2002; the Metropolitan Museum of New York, 2013; and the Pompidou, Paris, 2013.

His work is represented in the collection of the White Building, University of Michigan; the Midwest Museum of American Art, Elkhart, Indiana; and in the Saginaw Art Museum. He has taught at Merrimack Valley of Music and Art in Manchester, New Hampshire, and at the Fairlawn Community Center in New Jersey.

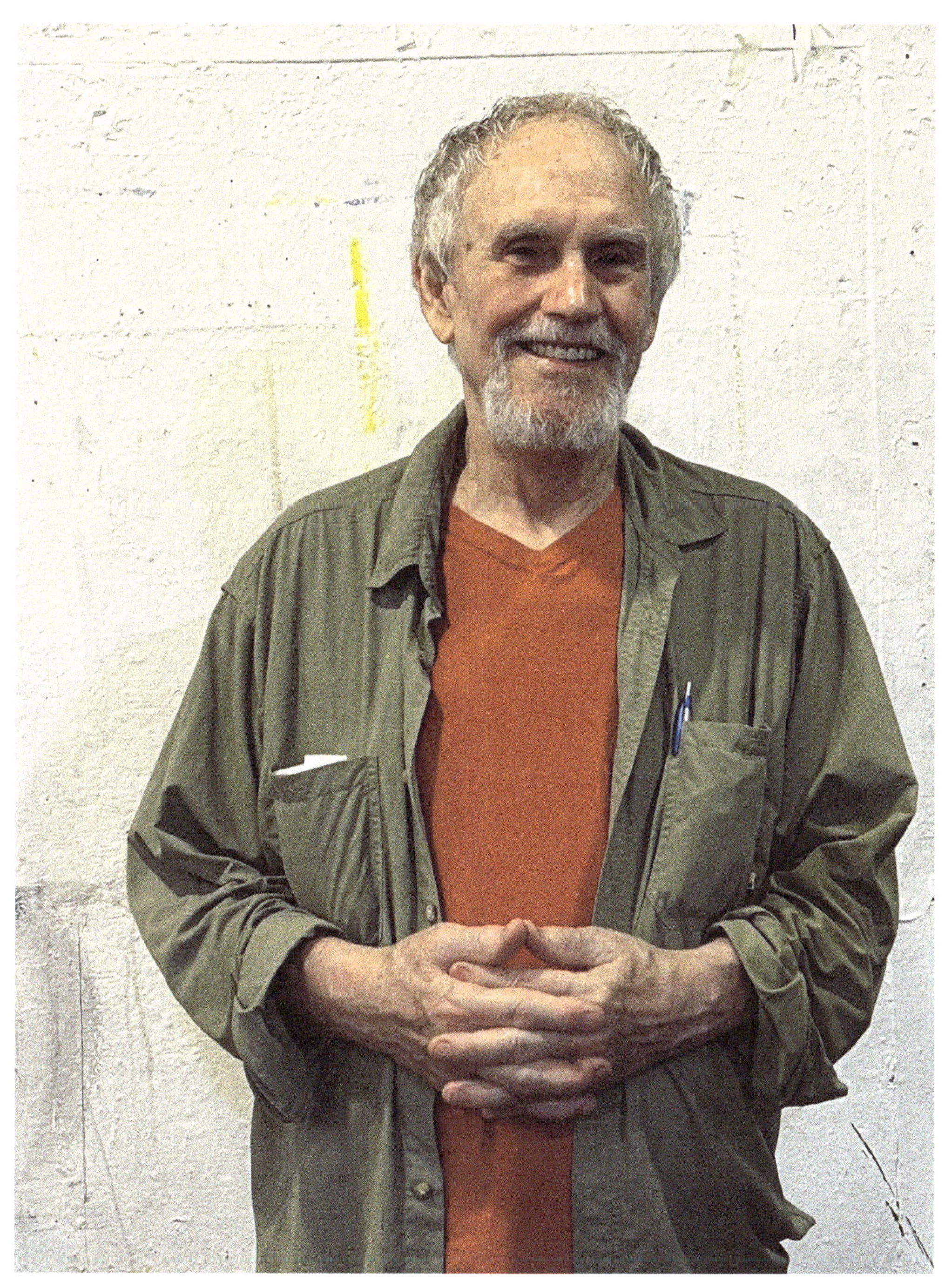

Frank O'Cain's web site

https://frank-ocain-yxxj.squarespace.com

www.ingramcontent.com/pod-product-compliance
Lightning Source LLC
LaVergne TN
LVHW081423110826
845149LV00010B/1844
9798988871705